Living, Healing
and # Tae Kwon Do

A Memoir to Inspire **Your Inner Warrior**

Living, Healing and Tae Kwon Do

Laura Di Franco, MPT

Brave Healer Productions

Living, Healing and Tae Kwon Do:
A Memoir to Inspire Your Inner Warrior

Laura Di Franco, MPT

ISBN: 978-1-7330738-0-6

Contents

Acknowledgments

This book is dedicated to all the teachers who have shown up in my life: my ex-husband, my children, my family, my friends, the friends I lost, my clients, my coaches, my neighbors, the authors of the books I've read, and my mom...thank you all for giving me the space to struggle and grow, for showing me the way, for loving me and letting go.

I'm grateful for the healing journey I've been on that has included all of you and has inspired me to write this book. I'm even grateful for the lost loves, the broken promises, and the failed jobs. I can see their place in the big picture now.

These are my stories of living, healing and Tae Kwon Do. I will be forever grateful to all the people who—through their patience, nonjudgmental teaching, and unwavering presence—have guided me. I hope that somehow I'll be able to give back as much as you have given to me, by living well and paying your lessons forward.

Mom, not only did you never doubt my passion, but you encouraged me, supported and guided me, advised me, and let me vent. Most of all, you loved me no matter what I said or did or who I was. You always have. I've always felt it. Thank you.

A special thank you to Jeanette MacDonald, the amazing artist who created me and that fabulous purple dragon on the front cover. Meeting Jeanette was one of the events of my life that made me believe in magic. Please find Jeanette at www.JeanetteMacDonaldArt.com.

Thanks to my book coach, Martha Bullen, for inspiring me to release this new edition of the book and take back a bit of my publishing power. Read about Martha at www.BullenPublishing-Services.com.

Thanks to my editor, Tammi Metzler, who helped make this new edition shine at a new level of sparkle! Find Tammi at www.WriteAssociate.com.

And thank you to Christy Collins at Constellation Book Services for designing a cover and insides for this book that made me more excited and proud than the first time.

Introduction

I stood in our spare room folding laundry one Saturday morning in July of 2007 and had the usual to-do list running through my head. I was still perspiring from my morning run, during which my multitasking brain had taken over. Along with figuring out my family's life schedule for the week, I was fairly certain I had also figured out world peace.

Having just woken up, my son came quietly into the room, rubbing his eyes and ducking under the t-shirt I was folding to wrap his arms around my waist and bury his head under my arm.

How lucky I was that I remembered to stop what I was doing (both physically and mentally) and hugged back, feeling his hot, sleepy forehead against my side. I cleared my mind of the many things that had cluttered it moments before and really felt that hug. I gave enough squeeze back that he knew I was "listening." I didn't let go until he was ready. We should all say good morning like that.

This was a precious moment. They are *all* precious. The stories you are about to read describe the journey that helped me to live each moment as precious, and that is my kind of Tae Kwon Do.

I thought about writing this book a few days before I was scheduled for a procedure to have a lump removed from my upper arm. In other words, in case I died on the table by some freak accident, I wanted my kids to have my version of the secrets to living. I wanted them to know that life has meaning and purpose, and I wanted

1

them to know my stories. Well, I never did get around to making that book happen in the four days before surgery, but since I did make it out alive, I thought I would give it a try.

I've always been excited about life and felt I wanted to motivate others to be excited about living it with passion. This is one of my biggest strengths. I've always felt this way but was limited by fear. The stories you're about to read include lessons I learned that allowed me to heal and transform into the truest expression of myself, of joy and love. They're stories of my passions and my sorrows.

I've studied books, practiced awareness, reflected and wrote about my experiences and relationships, and listened to many kinds of teachers, all of which have been critical to healing.

Starting in 2006, a few special teachers helped me to organize and process all the nuggets of my life into a path that created a new possibility for living more fiercely alive. I'm meant to share it.

I've learned to practice present moment awareness, and it's been a gift. Like you, I want happiness; I want love; I want wealth, health and success...and I want all these things for my family, too. I want us to have a life that's lived passionately and joyfully in each of its moments.

Something was preventing me from having this kind of life. My life felt difficult and tight and painful at times. I was stuck not only in fear but the kind of fear that made me feel small, constrained, hopeless and frustrated. It paralyzed me. I was in the middle of a really great life, and fear kept me from happiness.

My whole life has been about overcoming this kind of fear. Like many others, I felt better in my comfort zone. Why get risky when you can play it safe? But staying safe was costing me my health and my joy, and that cost became too high.

I felt exhausted and unhappy. I followed the rules (as in, everyone else's), didn't upset anybody, never spoke up, never said no, and started burning myself out. Somewhere along the line, I lost my voice, and that took a toll on me physically and mentally.

As I worked to heal, to understand and peel off the layers of old conditioned reactions and fear, I began to wake up and feel more alive. I had to figure out who I truly was, why I was on the planet, and why that mattered. I had to find a voice and learn to use it.

I found the passions that lit me up and then began pursuing those passions every day in some small way. I had to forgive and learn about love. I started taking Tae Kwon Do lessons and learned how to fight the inner demons (as well as get in kickass shape).

I healed with acupuncture, myofascial release, and workshops on communication. I healed in the presence of friends and teachers who listened. Ultimately, I learned how to do something with my fear instead of being paralyzed by it.

Every time I managed to overcome my fear and take action, I felt physically lighter, stronger, faster and more able to speak from my heart. I noticed everything around me and was able to center myself in the moment, which made my response to the world feel alive and joyful. I was able to detach from the outcome and see things as just what was, not good or bad. I was able to feel fear—the physical reality of it in my body, the thoughts that invaded my mind—and act and speak anyway. This was huge.

The surge of creative energy that I've experienced as a result of waking up and peeling off the layers has been the kind that will change things in a big way.

There are people who have had to deal with much more severe trauma than I've ever had to. I think about them a lot. I hope they find healers to guide them. I hope they find the courage to reach out. I hope they find their Tae Kwon Do.

Part of my reason for being is to help give people another idea of healing. All lives are a work in progress, and yours and mine are no different. Perfection is not the goal. This book is a peek into how I've done this life and keep doing it, moment by moment, living, healing and kicking my way through...

Tae Kwon Do Belt Color Meanings

There're several books and websites that talk about the meanings of the belt colors. In Tae Kwon Do, there are two governing federations, the International Tae Kwon-Do Federation and the World Taekwondo Federation. They each have their own system of forms, rules and guidelines.

Depending on who your instructor is and who their instructor was, you will practice under one of these sets of guidelines. At Gentle East Taekwondo, where I practice, we follow the ITF rules, and the following definitions come from there.

The ITF website talks about Tae Kwon Do being a way of life. It states, "To demonstrate the value of ITF Tae KwonDo as a way of life, we must teach all facets of ITF Tae KwonDo, including the Do." In this case, "do" means "the way." It goes on to say, "The ultimate purpose in life is the search for happiness...Many people suffer because they do not have the proper value system that leads to a balanced life and happiness."

My journey has been about this exact search. I hadn't read any of the history of belt color meanings before doing this writing, and yet I have experienced a transformation that has ultimately led to balance and happiness.

This was not because our instructors talked about it or taught it with those exact words. They taught the "do" with their patience, skill and experience, as well as by letting us find our own way through. When I take a step back and try to fit the whole experience into my field of vision, I begin to wonder why they don't write some kind of self-help Tae Kwon Do book (maybe that is what I just did) or advertise it for what it really is: a way to experience life and find its true meaning and purpose. If they did, more people might sign up for lessons.

All of that being said, here are the belt color meanings:

White: The color white in Tae Kwon Do means innocence and no knowledge of Tae Kwon Do.

Yellow: The color yellow stands for the earth in which the seed of Tae Kwon Do has been planted and takes root. It's about laying the foundation of Tae Kwon Do.

Green: Green symbolizes the seed sprouting and reaching toward the sun. Your knowledge of Tae Kwon Do is building.

Blue: The color blue symbolizes the sky toward which the plant is growing and reaching. Your knowledge is growing, and your skills are being fine-tuned.

Red: Red means danger—the student is warned to practice control of his or her movements.

Black: The color black in Tae Kwon Do describes a maturity and proficiency in Tae Kwon Do, an imperviousness to darkness and fear, and a new beginning.

A Beginning

E*very story has to start somewhere. What's the beginning of yours?*
My beginning is somewhere in the middle, as an almost-forty-something wife and mother trying to figure out how to be happy and healthy. Up to that point, I'd done everything by the book. I went to school and became a professional with a good-paying job—check. I met a good-looking, hard-working, honest guy and got married—check. I ran three marathons—check. We had two children, one boy and one girl—check. I opened my own private physical therapy practice—check.

Happy yet? No, for some reason. *Why the hell not?* one inner voice said. *You ought to be grateful for all the wonderful things you have, for all of your accomplishments!*

I know, I know, I thought to myself. *I am.*

So why did I feel this way? Like something was missing? Like everything until this point had been for someone else besides me?

In my beginning, like many, I busied my life and the lives of my family with things to do to fill our time, to make us happy. I started to think about getting the kids involved in some activities because, well, it would be good for them. I wanted to get us all out of the house and engaged in life because that is what happy families should do.

My husband and I thought martial arts might be good for our son, because he was shy and a little bit sensitive. We took him to a dojang one day, walked up to the stairs where the entrance to the

7

school was and were about to go in and check it out when we all heard the yells coming from the room below.

"Hiiiya!"

I guess the sounds of the students' kihaps scared my little dude, because he turned around and refused to take another step. Strike one.

Later, we saw the listings for Tae Kwon Do and karate in our YMCA catalog. My kids both attended the childcare program in the building where these classes were held, so we were all used to seeing the kids, parents and teachers in their uniforms in the hallways.

"Hey, bud, let's go watch a Tae Kwon Do class at the Y," I encouraged.

We would peek into the gym now and again to check it out. Karate was on Friday nights, and that wasn't going to fit into our schedule, so that left Tae Kwon Do.

My son and I walked out after watching a class together.

"So, what do you think, buddy?" I asked.

"I'll do it if you do it, Mom," he replied, looking up at me with a grin.

Fair enough, I thought. "Deal!" I said. And my husband could bring our daughter to the pee wee gymnastics class on the same day, even better! We planned to do a trial class that next week.

My journal entry dated January 31, 2006, read:

I have signed us up for some YMCA programs. Dani and Dad will do Daddy 'n' Me Gymnastics, and Jon and I are in Tae Kwon Do! I'm nervous but so excited!

Journal entry March 12, 2006

I wanted to write again tonight about Tae Kwon Do. Jonathan and I started our class at the YMCA last weekend. I think we both have a new sport! I am weirdly drawn to this class. Masters Holloway, Hathway, and McDermott were there to teach us the forms and the bow. During the first class, master McDermott, the female teacher, warmed us up. Forty jumping jacks, fifty double leg lifts, fifty push-ups, splits...my abs were sore for three or four days. I hurt myself, but I didn't realize it until later. The Wednesday after, I made a point to do an intense weight workout, including working on the double leg lifts and push-ups. I really feel ready to get into awesome shape. My lower abs hurt a little on Wednesday, but not a ton. So we went back for our second session, decked out in our doboks (uniform), did our warm-up, and started to do some of the leg lifts again, but this time there was sharp pain in my right lower abs, and I couldn't work through it. So now I hope it heals so I can continue to work hard and learn some new things. Both Jonathan and I jammed our toes trying to kick the bag. Only I had already jammed mine the week before, so now I have a really jammed toe! It hurt so bad that I had trouble running this morning but felt better toward the end of the run.

I have had so much fun in just two sessions watching Jon learning something new, and he is really good at it. He is so serious about what he is doing, but he is also having fun, which is exactly how I am feeling. We already have a very close bond, but doing this with him is very cool. We have an interest in common, and I really hope that we will be able to continue this, improve and get our black belts!

(By the way, you don't get a black belt; you earn it.)

More from March 12, 2006

Taekwondo is very athletic. It makes my hands sweat. What is up with that? Jonathan even said something about that too. It is inspiring me to be motivated to improve my flexibility and strength. Really, my secret passion is to be Uma. Except I don't need to be blonde.

The whole fighting thing scares me. I am not sure what it is I think I am getting into. I suppose one could practice without having to spar. My little guy in his uniform is a sight. He is the smallest guy in the class, but probably has the most spirit. I feel very proud to be there with him.

We learned the opening tee up, the bow, junbi stance, kicks: front stretch, front snap, abduction, adduction, side, 45-degree, back, single, double and triple punch. We learned knowledge of the feet and hands. I think that we could be good at this. I think this could be something that I can strive for, that I can do without having to worry about my insides (except for my abs now). Funny, though, how this has brought back the old pregnancy injury to let me be aware that it isn't fully healed. What I think is that I needed to step up my conditioning...and this is the way. This will be a way to heal.

Journal entry May 1, 2006

Taekwondo is going very well. I still love it. I am working out one time a week at the Y doing weights, push-ups and abs. I am getting stronger. I can do sixty leg lifts now and forty partial push-ups. My arms and legs are looking good.

We finished the ninth week of Tae Kwon Do...now we will switch to Thursday nights for the summer. I still want to do a second class a week, but it is not in the cards right now. I have been reading a Tae Kwon Do book, and they talk about being able to get to black belt in two years. I figured that just has to be the ultimate timing, getting a black belt for my fortieth birthday.

(Turns out that the "they" I was referring to had one idea of how long it should take. I hadn't thought of asking the most important source, my own instructor.)

Journal entry May 6, 2006

Jonathan and I started our second session of Tae Kwon Do on Thursday night. We switched from Saturdays so we could plan things on the weekends, mainly camping. The Thursday class is big, with twenty-one people there this week. The class started different-ly with a lot of talk...not as formal as usual. Masters Holloway and McDermott were there. Toward the end, we did the bags. The 45's / personal best. I ruined my feet, to make a long story short. Bruised! And I pulled something in my lower leg. I would have done more than forty, but I will have another chance I am sure.

Master McDermott told me we would test soon. Jon is so excited to get a stripe! Me too!

When I found these entries in my journal, I chuckled to myself. Why would someone love an activity that in the first few classes caused an abdominal tear, jammed toe, bruised feet and a pulled leg?

Ha! If I only knew then what I know now, that list would expand to a torn calf, bleeding lip, whiplashed neck, more than a dozen bruised knees and elbows and an almost-broken rib.

(Mom, please chill as you read this; I'm being careful.)

Not only did we go back, but we were hooked! Hooked on what, you might wonder? Pain? I'm tempted to say "no, not pain," but I am changing my mind. Pain sometimes lets you know you are alive in a "what doesn't kill you makes you stronger" kind of way. I needed to feel alive. I was trying to fill a hole that I didn't even know was gaping inside of me.

I remember in our first class, Jonathan and I were lined up off to the side in the gym with a few other plain-clothed students. Master McDermott was breaking us in. We were practicing the side kick. I loved Tae Kwon Do that very first day. *Loved it*. Every part of me, as I sweat through my clothes, was excited about it.

Master McDermott stepped down the line of us one by one, holding out the paddle and checking out our kicks, fine-tuning our techniques. She asked me, "You've done this before, right?"

"No," I answered, secretly thrilled that she would make a comment like that and thinking, maybe in another life?

The exercises, kicks and movements all felt strangely comfortable and caused an instant attraction (addiction). It wouldn't be until a couple belts later that we would realize just what we were getting ourselves into. Part of what I was drawn to without completely knowing it that first time or two was how Tae Kwon Do demanded my attention to the present moment. *This is what Eckhart was talking about in his book,* A New Earth, I thought. I was having an experience of what it was like to be immersed in the moment, in joy.

Thinking back to my first writing about Tae Kwon Do, I'd hoped our journey would *get* us a black belt. I didn't know what that meant back then; I just felt the energy of it in that very first class, thanks to Master M and Master Holloway.

Honestly, now I feel that you don't really, truly know what you are getting into until well into your red belt. By then, I felt there was no turning back. I'm so grateful we decided to go for it and that I decided to journal about it for the last six years.

I am honored to share my journey with all of you. I encourage you to find your passions, whatever form they take. For those of you who are curious about Tae Kwon Do, take a class. Don't be afraid! You will love it or hate it; either way, it's all good.

This journey for me has been about living and healing, not just surviving. Tae Kwon Do has been part of the path, along with other teachers and healers that guided me. I've learned that the ideas of transformation, healing, and living with joy are real, achievable, and worthy pursuits. I've been able to redefine what it means to be healthy.

I try to remind myself daily what it means to be truly healthy, that it's not just the absence of disease. The discipline of Tae Kwon Do requires this daily due diligence. I check in with myself often, practice awareness, and try to honor my body, mind, and emotions by noticing them and paying attention.

I pursue my passions in my work and in my play. I've begun to make work my play. I practice these things both in Tae Kwon Do class and out. I practice not being attached to the outcome by taking an action and then letting go and trusting, come what may. I remember who I am...and then I go back to doing the laundry.

I even managed to overcome my laundry resentment through this process, which made me increasingly grateful for everything in my life. I fold now not with irritation but feeling happy to own so many clothes in the first place. That might sound corny, but it changed my entire way of being around stuff I didn't like to do. Being grateful was only part of my beginning, but it was an important part. More on living in gratitude later.

Use these pages to record your thoughts about the question at the beginning of this chapter...where does your story begin?

Identity

If you stripped away all your labels (mother, daughter, wife, friend, professional, athlete, etc.), all the roles that you identify with as who you are, what would you be left with? Whom would you be?

In my twenties and thirties, I existed in my career and in my running. I was attached to the idea of who I was through what I did and what I achieved, in an unhealthy way. It would take a trauma and resulting huge loss of identity to force me to begin to learn who I really was and feel alive again.

Following is a little bit of my past. I write this as a memorial to the person who lived and survived in her running B.T. (before Tae Kwon Do).

Journal entry May 2, 2000

One day, after rambling on and on to my husband about what marathon I wanted to run next, what sort of training I wanted to do this year, and how I was hoping he would help me with the baby so I could meet with my running group on Saturdays, he asked me, "Why do you like running so much?"

The question surprised and delighted me. My husband, so obviously not a runner, wanted me to tell him what I liked about running, the one thing that I felt partially defined me as a person. Now was my chance to get him hooked too, because obviously my passion would be contagious.

Instead of trying to sell running to him like a used car, I gave him an answer that came from my heart, that part of me who was a runner. He got to know his wife a little bit better.

"It's the way I feel after a run. It's the feeling of being in the best shape I've ever been in. It's the time I get to myself to think and meditate. It's the time I get to know my runner friends and laugh and joke with them. It's freedom. It's the smell of the trees and the touch of the wind. It's the squish of new running shoes. It's being in nature and feeling like a part of it. It's being able to eat chocolate without guilt."

I think he might have been surprised by the length of my answer, thinking that there couldn't be all that much to it. There's so much to it for me that I always thought everyone should love it as much as I do. But part of the reason why running is special for some is that it's not special for everyone. Regardless, I was happy someone asked me that question. We runners know why we run. Sometimes we mistakenly think everyone else knows, too.

I needed to feel special, and running, specifically marathons, was how I was showing the world that I could be outstanding. Achieving was important; it defined excellence for me.

At my martial arts school, Gentle East Taekwondo, we have to turn in an essay when we take our test for the next stripe or belt. The essay can be about anything we choose, and the younger kids are allowed to draw a picture instead of writing. We're not allowed to be promoted without the essay.

When I found out about the essay requirement, I was so excited. I'd always loved to write. Now I would get to write about Tae Kwon Do, my new passion! A version of this piece on figuring out who I am ended up being the essay I turned in to Master Holloway for my first exam for the yellow stripe.

Yellow Stripe Essay

I thought I knew who I was. Then I had kids. The changes forced me to realize I wasn't the person I thought I was. They forced me to wonder who the hell I really was. Mother, friend, runner, physical therapist, wife, athlete—among other things, I suppose.

The piece that always kept me in balance was my running. Running gives me time to myself, to think, meditate, sweat...it keeps me in great shape, is very convenient, and doesn't require much equipment. I am a runner. When I ran a marathon, I felt like Wonder Woman. So I ran two more. The commitment it took to train was intense, but when I crossed the finish line, it was all worth it. Now I was a marathoner, a physical therapist, a wife, and a friend, in that order. This defined me. I had not become a mother yet.

The day my son was born, I felt the miracle. The raw physical bond was overwhelming. I was a mother now, and all the other things would fall in line behind that. Including runner. The expectation that I had to keep in shape and continue running was high. I would keep the part of me that maintained order and balance, kept me sane and kept me fit, no matter what. I would prioritize. I would not lose that part of my identity. Then I did.

I trained and ran a half marathon some months after giving birth and with some difficulties managed to run a couple more 10Ks. My body did not cooperate.

I had sustained some damage during the birthing process that caused a bladder, uterine and rectal prolapse. I remember standing, pacing in the hospital room, just my husband and I, left to labor by ourselves for a while.

Jonathan's head had dropped, and I swear I couldn't stand with my legs together. I rested my forehead on my husband's chest, burst into tears and said, "I don't think I can do this."

I just couldn't imagine it happening, that baby making it out. The opening I had been familiar with for 32 years at that point just wasn't going to be big enough.

Eighteen hours, a pair of really large forceps and some third-degree tears later, Jonathan was out. They really don't prepare you for that type of scenario. For many years, I could not handle my husband telling his version of the story that included how the doctor, bracing himself by placing both of his feet up on the bed, played tug of war with Jonathan's head, using salad tongs, and then finally pulled him out. It's no wonder that in the healing world, they call birth the first real trauma.

I ran on through some gross kinds of pain, knowing—or maybe hoping—I would heal. I began seriously thinking about running another marathon after my daughter was born. That was it! Two kids. Done. Check. Now I can get my body back, my running back, myself back.

The constant effort to redefine myself during this time of my life was exasperating. Why was this so difficult? Why wasn't I healing? Wasn't I meant to be a runner and an athlete? Why was there still pain? I could not check this box and move on.

On and off for about five years, I endured this struggle. Then I began to push less, listen to my body more, and sort of give up on the idea of any more serious running, at the same time not knowing how I was supposed to fill the void that I had just created. I was sad, and some days I was outright depressed. If only I could run another marathon, then I would be me again.

Jonathan had just turned six the year we started practicing Tae Kwon Do at the Y. This intense, powerful, athletic, interesting sport lit a fire inside of me.

After beginning the classes, I reconnected with some part of myself that began to fill the void. The athlete in me was challenged again and excited. I was motivated to see where my limits were and push them.

There was no struggle with my body as I practiced the forms. None of the old pain. I felt strong and powerful. I was learning a form of self-defense. This particular gift of Tae Kwon Do was important to me.

Something that came with being a mother was a vulnerability that I didn't expect, an excruciating vulnerability and desperate need to protect my child. It came with the fear that I was not capable of protecting him. It was both lack of control and feeling unable to physically defend myself. I couldn't do a whole lot about the control thing, but I could learn to fight. Tae Kwon Do helped me face that fear and act in spite of it.

What I received when my son and I stepped into the dojang for the first time was so much greater than I expected. I was given the gift of hope, the exhilaration of feeling passionate about a sport again.

I had a rekindling of some of my natural physical and mental strengths that would be enhanced by learning this new art. The feelings about it have been so overwhelming that I have second-guessed myself at times, wondering if my usual Type A behavior is taking over, but this feels different. You can't mistake real passion. It lights up a room.

I also began to understand the idea of attachment. I was so attached to the way I identified myself as a runner and the good feelings I had when I ran that when I found myself unable to run, I felt depressed and trapped by my own thoughts of pain, anger, and sadness. I didn't see a bigger picture.

I only felt the loss of a huge piece of who I was. I spent much time reliving the experiences of the past, trying to figure out why I was feeling this way, and focusing on my leftover anger and sadness. Nobody really understood. They were waiting for me to snap out of it.

It was so difficult to redefine myself as a mother. I was pissed at the doctors, disappointed that the experience of being pregnant and giving birth was nothing I had dreamed of or hoped for, and sick and exhausted the rest of the time. That didn't leave any room for new passion.

I had identified with and attached to myself as a runner because that's what was bringing passion into my life then. It was a release, a kind of escape that was something just for me. Once I could no longer run, I didn't see any other way to get that relief; I just felt the loss.

Why weren't my roles as a mother or a wife—or even as a physical therapist—as impactful as running was to my identity at that point in my life? Because they felt like work. I hadn't been able to meld all the areas of my life together to bring me joy. I was afraid of expressing myself to my husband, worried about doing everything wrong as a mother, and working so many hours in my job that I exhausted myself. On the other hand, running was joy. And then running hurt.

Now, these many years later, I am so passionate about Tae Kwon Do that I've been inspired to write a book about it. I can see clearly that the experiences I endured that I called "bad" were actually a gift.

What if I had never had children; what if the birth of my first child was uneventful, without injury; or what if I had fully recovered and resumed my running activities as planned, training for the next marathon? I would probably have never discovered Tae Kwon Do.

At the time, the events of the moment were devastating, not to mention painful. I struggled a lot. Cried a lot. The big picture is impossible to see in our moments of despair. We must remember who we are, and it is none of those things we identify with so much.

We can sit and observe the reactions, emotions, and drama in our lives and begin to wonder who it is that is observing it. If we are awake to it, then who is it that's awake, aware, and observing?

We are way more powerful than all of our reactions and emotions.

I don't know what my current situation holds for me. I'm blind to its purpose, so I try not to judge. I have faith that the events of my life are meant to be, and I'm aware that I have choices. I rest in knowing that it's all good. I'm bigger than all of it. I am none of it. It's a mystery, and I can enjoy not knowing for now.

I do know that my path led me into the dojang that day, unaware, just following my son into class. I get to look back six years later in wonderment. Amazing. Not random. That I'm sure of!

The poems on the following pages were written during the time that running defined me. These small pieces of my soul shone through, and I lived for these moments, like I now live to practice my Tae Kwon Do.

About Running

I came inside from my morning run
And my husband asked, "What were you doing?"
I replied, "Writing a poem."

Running
in the Rain
makes me feel tough.

I am flashing back to my soccer days
when games were rain or shine.
We would race through soggy fields,
slamming the ball through mud puddles,
looking up through dread-locked bangs that
were matted to our foreheads to see where the ball went,
only to realize that it was still at our feet, stuck in a hole.

I was wet and dirty and tough.

Now I am running in the pouring rain
on the streets through my neighborhood because my husband and kids
are napping and I have some time for exercise.
The drops drip off the trees and bounce off the brim of my cap...

I am wet and sweaty and tough.

I love it!

Breathe...

The world is full of souls
trying to take a breath.
The world doesn't give us
much room to breathe

with obstacles
like sadness and fear
crowding our hearts.

But without these things
we wouldn't realize
love or hope or happiness.

Come on soul
push the walls away from you
make room to breathe.
Love and hope and happiness
are waiting to fill up your lungs.

I would draft these poems in my mind as I ran and write them down when I returned home. I think back and feel this poem. It's the idea of Yin and Yang. We can't know bliss without knowing suffering.

Taekwondo has allowed me to continue to write, letting the stuff of my soul be expressed. I have asked myself the question, "What do you like so much about Tae Kwon Do?" just so I can answer to my heart's content.

Being able to do this has helped me uncover who I truly am, to understand that who I am isn't only the roles I play or labels I put on myself. It has helped me to uncover a power inside of me to be myself, and be anything I want to be.

Writing helps me express who I am in the best, most authentic way, without having to be afraid of speaking. Now I'm realizing I need to speak it too, so that others might know who I am.

How do you uncover who you truly are?

Use these pages to record your thoughts about the questions at the beginning and end of each chapter...

Heaven and Earth

What pieces of your past, as you look now retrospectively, were pivotal in shaping the person you are today?

I believe an unapologetically positive attitude is what helped shape the journey of healing, learning, and exploration I've been on. Optimism was my default mindset and served me well through those years.

I look back at a picture of myself during my Tae Kwon Do yellow stripe test, and now I can teach that young student: place your feet a little wider apart, lock your back knee, tuck your back fist at your belt so that your palm faces up, turn your chest and shoulders toward the front, and punch down and center.

It's fun to be able to correct myself in this picture, as it shows me what I've learned. Man, does that uniform sparkle. The first form in Tae Kwon Do that we learn is called Chon-Ji, which means "heaven and earth."

I remember how much I enjoyed getting my uniform, called a dobok in Korean, and how it made me feel like I belonged to something again. It was the same feeling I used to have when I played soccer in college.

I would set out my uniform the night before a game and stare at it, imagining and visualizing my performance, in a sort of ritual. The uniform symbolized belonging, experience, being part of a bigger picture, dedication, sacrifice, and a certain level of achievement.

Those feelings seemed to rush back the day I put on my dobok and wrapped my belt around my waist. The feeling was different from being one member of a team, though. It was bigger somehow. I not only belonged to the Gentle East Taekwondo school, I was part of this really big team of martial artists in the world. I was part of a new way of living.

I was always a glass-half-full (a.k.a. very positive) person, even back in my college years. The coaches and teachers I had until that point were all about attitude, and that shaped me well. This was along with having a mom who told me to do my best and that she would love me no matter what.

I visualized myself scoring a goal, or blocking a shot. I wrote and reflected on my life and what I could do to improve. I dreamed up goals and made lists to check off. I imagined what my future would be like, being an athlete and maintaining my career as a physical therapist. I even took the Tony Robbins course, *Unlimited Power*, as a twenty-something.

Tony talked about turning fear into power. He used—get ready for this—board breaking as a metaphor for breaking through anything that has stopped you in your life.

A journal entry from my *Unlimited Power* notebook:

"Board breaking. Why are we doing this? Board breaking is a great metaphor for breaking through and taking action. You are going to break through the wood, and it is going to represent a breaking through of those beliefs and fears that have limited you in the past. Look at the wood as a solid belief, a solid limitation, and you are breaking through it."

I believe having a positive attitude has saved me at times from getting sucked into the black hole of despair. It's allowed me to question those solid beliefs I had drilled into me from a young age.

I always knew that there were ways to do life that would not be about fear and limitation but rather about the opposites of that. I wanted to learn how to do it that way. Thinking positively just felt better most the time. It comes from being grateful. It's full of hope and love.

Think of the alternative. Actually, don't do that. Don't waste your precious time, not one more moment of it, thinking negatively.

I loved a piece of Dr. Wayne Dyer's book *Excuses Begone* that went something like this: "If you are worrying about something and you are not 100% sure that the outcome will be X (positive), but you are also not 100% sure that the outcome will by Y (negative), in the mean time, keep the thoughts in your mind about X. Think positively in the mean time. At the very least, your waiting will be more enjoyable."

If you end up getting sucked into the black hole, and we all do, hopefully at some point you'll realize it's really dark in there and snap yourself out of it. Being able to change your thoughts at will is a skill worth mastering. Attitude is everything.

Journal entry June 14, 2006

Taekwondo test tomorrow night! Jonathan will be great...he really knows his stuff.

Journal entry July 14, 2006

Learned the new form for Tae Kwon Do last night! On our way to the yellow belt. The new form has twenty-one moves. I tried to write them down when I got home, but I'm not sure I got it all right. We sure are having fun with this, though.

Journal entry July 20, 2006

Jonathan cried today when Ms. McDermott asked him to do the form. I felt so bad, like it was my fault. That sounds silly. But I want so badly for Jonathan to keep enjoying this. I felt bad and sad.

These are the times that you can relate to when you remember someone saying that having children is like wearing your heart on your sleeve. You think you know what they are talking about before you have kids, and then you know what they are talking about after you have them. Vulnerability is a difficult thing to talk about and an even more difficult thing to feel.

My yellow belt essay on September 23, 2006, ended up being a poem:

The yellow stripe
In Tae Kwon Do
Nineteen moves
You must know.

Starting off with
Our first moves
We kick, we punch
It is all so new.
We've practiced our combos
And we know Chon-Ji
We can't wait for
Master Holloway to see.

Now we are up
It's our turn to show
All the new moves
That we must know.

But who knew this testing
Would be like this
It's just nerves but
They're hard to miss.

Then we finish
And see we have passed

It seemed to go
All so fast.

We have our stripe
A handshake and praise
We can now look forward
To the yellow belt days.

Our yellow belt
In Tae Kwon Do!
Twenty-one moves
Is a lot to know.

With practice and training
We grow stronger
We have the endurance
To last longer.

We know our kicks
And form by heart
If only I could remember
How to start!

Sometimes testing
Is hard to do
When all eyes
Are watching you.

But when you're done
You feel great!
With a new belt
And a handshake.

Then a smile
Is hard to hide

Your heart is bursting
Full of pride

The next new moves
Remain to be seen
I can't wait
To get to green!

Journal entry September 23, 2006:

Had our yellow belt test today. We did great. Because there are so many students in the classes now, we went to a separate room with Master Holloway to test. It was better than the first test we took, nerves-wise. I wonder if that is because I was used to it or because of Robin (my acupuncturist). Jonathan did very well too, despite his father stressing out on him about not practicing enough. I was surprised that we were the only two people testing today. It was great to get our yellow belts.

Are you half full or half empty?

Use these pages to record your thoughts about the questions at the beginning and end of this chapter...

Beyond Magic

Who are the healers and teachers in your life that showed you what you were capable of?

The year I started Tae Kwon Do was also the year I met Robin, my acupuncturist. My whole world began to change as she gently guided me on what seemed later like a magical journey of energy, feeling and intuition.

Robin was part of my heaven. She taught me about feeling heaven while my feet stayed grounded on the earth. My life wouldn't be what it is without her.

I no longer consider it a coincidence that Robin came into my life the same year I started Tae Kwon Do. There are parts of life I wonder how I would have survived without Robin, and parts of Tae Kwon Do that wouldn't have happened at all without her. I also believe Robin held my marriage together for a really long time.

Robin is made up of part love and part magic. She would tell you that the magic is just baby stuff. More later about the magic of healing.

Journal entry May 31, 2006

I started seeing an acupuncturist a few weeks ago. Robin. Calling her an acupuncturist is really not quite sufficient. She's a healer. She's helping me, and I wanted to make some notes about our session today.

We went right to Jonathan's birth, but I'm realizing it's deeper. My heart, old fear. Dad. Anger. Fear mostly. I'm repressing the hurt of my heart.

Low back pain eased quickly by the time I was driving after the session. Felt dazed (blurred vision and tired eyes) the rest of the day. Tired. Tired eyes.

Robin, you are my little crazy angel.

Talked a lot, have been talking a lot about my daughter. She is a reflection of me, of my chaos. Being able to love more. Yeah, that is what this is all about. I don't need to know what it's about. I just need to feel. Better times with her dad means the discipline issues will go away.

Today, as I felt the fear come out, I felt my belly pulling up and in. I actually felt it. I have been compromising my healing by playing into other people's fears. Lump in my throat, can't talk, afraid. It's okay, I'm here now to help you.

This journal entry about Robin is a little all over the place. I was feeling the effects of being broken open physically and energetically. Core pieces of hurt were being uncovered, and I was attempting to sort it all out. Some things are better when you just sit back and enjoy the ride.

I have since referred many of my friends and clients to Robin and have made several attempts to describe both what she has done for me and what she's all about. It's very difficult to find the words, but I have to smile as I reread my journal from that year. It explained it.

She's helped me peel back the layers of my life, the ones that have prevented me from shining. She pulled me out of myself. She has done that with talking and acupuncture and love. She has listened with full attention to every single story of my life, including every Tae Kwon Do tale. She's my witness. She's given me the confidence to spar. The kind I needed to feel so that fear of hurting myself wouldn't get in the way.

I'm eternally grateful to her for giving me the ability to live like I do today, with passion, hope, wonder and appreciation. I'm thrilled every time I remember the day I walked into the Bethesda Co-op and decided to stop at the bulletin board to scan for an acupuncturist. I pulled her card off the board and called the next day. Here I stand six years later in a life of real joy. Thank you and I love you, Robin.

Acupuncture is something I began to dabble with around 1999 when I was desperate to find a cure for morning sickness. The Eastern philosophy of medicine and healing resonates with me. It's direct, gentle, and holistic. It's mind and body and spirit. It's preventive but gets to a deep layer of your being where the healing can happen, so it goes beyond just prevention.

It helps you unblock the healing energy in your body. Chinese acupuncture dates back about 5,000 years. It was created to provide a system for the creation and maintenance of health. Its practitioners look at a person as a mind/body/spirit being. Acupuncturists believe there's a life force called "chi," or energy, and it flows through us in a balanced way. If the chi is not flowing well, we become ill.

Back to my journey toward acupuncture. Pregnant and desperate not to puke one more day, I was determined to feel better so I could function. I'd heard acupuncture might help, and it definitely took an edge off. I later sought out another acupuncturist who I heard dealt with allergies. I had a list of strange food sensitivities that nobody had been able to explain. My second acupuncturist, Jake, had a method of evaluation and treatment for it, the first person I had met who had a plan.

Lastly, after Danielle was born, my immune system was shot. Along with the normal exhaustion that comes with parents of a newborn baby, I was sick every three months with every kind of "itis" you can think of. My body couldn't fight the germs. *If I have to take one more antibiotic, I'm going to shoot myself*, I thought.

That was the year I met Robin. In the five or six years since I've met her, I have not had to take an antibiotic for an infection. Not once. That isn't even the icing.

My sleep is better, my digestion is calmer, my injuries heal with some kind of magical speed, and I love my life. That last one is the icing.

Nobody walks into an acupuncturist's office and says, "I would like to love my life, please." They say, "Can you do anything for this pain in my back?" Which, speaking of, the time I hurt my back, the pain was gone the day after my session with her.

I now put down Robin's name when I'm filling out forms that ask for a primary physician. Nobody's asked me about it yet. We all know they don't read what we spend twenty minutes writing down in the waiting room anyway.

To give you an appreciation for what I feel after an acupuncture session—and sometimes just leading up to one and a couple days after one—I need to try to describe the way I feel energy in my body. A difficult task because it is different for everyone.

Even if the sensations are the same, the way people describe them can be different. There are two ways I feel things happening when I'm with Robin. One is during conversation. When someone is listening to what you are saying—*really* listening with their whole self, mind, body, and spirit—they are listening to your words but they are also listening to your heart. Robin does this by using her own grounded, centered heart energy.

Robin listens in this way. She's present for every word. You can *feel* it. She's there to witness your words, your emotions, your body language, your reactions, and the way you do the dance of telling your story.

She sits with it and responds with a mix of intuition and love. I feel heard and understood and loved at the same time, no matter what I've said. When she listens like that, there's a perceptible shift inside of me, in my energy, in the way I feel as I sit there across from her.

Sometimes I feel the tightness in my chest and the lump in my throat, and I cannot help but cry. Sometimes a light bulb goes off, and a lightness envelops me. There have been times when I have begun to know what I want to talk about just minutes before our session as I'm driving in my car to see her. It's like my body and mind are preparing for the healing they're about to do. I know very few people who listen in this way. It's a gift beyond words to have someone in my life like this.

The other way I feel things happening is when I'm on Robin's table actually getting acupuncture. The sensations that would occur when the needles were in my body were very weird at first, until I began recognizing them and integrating what I was feeling on the table with what we had talked about and my knowledge of the flow of energy in the body.

I've felt a rush of heat and/or cold in my limbs. I've felt a cool blue ball of light in my pelvis. I've felt the feeling of being very small and afraid along with the sensations of deep sadness in my heart. I've fallen into another state of consciousness that I best describe as part sleep and part daydream.

There have been a couple of sessions where I was aware in my mind but lost the sensation of my body on the table, like everything was melting together as one. She calls these sensations the hypnagogic state. Who knew there was a word for it?

You might be wondering about what I'm describing if you have never felt anything like this before, so I encourage you to be open and interested in the possibility that there is a way to shift and move our energy for healing, other than what we have been taught by a Western system of medicine all of our lives. For me, this realization was a dream come true, as the Western medical system had only traumatized me up until then.

The work I've done with Robin has helped me to speak with the most difficult people in my life from a place in my heart. This means that my conversations with the difficult people are changing from me reacting, defending myself, and trying to be right, to me being able to listen to them and respond from a deeper place of compassion and understanding.

It's hard to not want to be right all the time. It takes practice to speak from this deeper heart space. It requires a level of presence I hadn't been used to tapping into. I still don't remember to do it all the time; just ask my ex-husband.

I've morphed my own healing practice because of what I've learned through my sessions with Robin and the other healers in the myofascial and craniosacral worlds. I work differently because of my experiences, and I can be a living example. When I heal, I make space for someone else's healing. What a gift. I'm going to explain a little more about my own healing practice in the next chapter.

And in case you're wondering, yes, sometimes the acupuncture needles hurt. But not for long.

Who or what helped you shape your attitude about life?

Use these pages to record your thoughts about the questions at the beginning and end of this chapter...

Who I Am Is What I Do

ow do you make a living? Do you love what you do?

HSince I chose a healing profession as my career, it's natural that this part of my life was a journey unto itself. I went from eager student to licensed physical therapist to experienced physical therapist to healer. It was the transformation to healer that had the most impact in my life.

Once upon a time, I was sitting in the middle of a continuing education class, and, after noticing the students were getting frustrated about not understanding the technique the instructor was demonstrating, he stopped and said, "Listen, folks, who I am is not what I do. At the end of the day, I can leave all of this and enjoy my life and pay attention to all the things that matter."

I get that by saying that, he was trying to make us all relax a little and drop some of the performance anxiety. I questioned it, though. Until that point, who I was *definitely* was what I did for a living and what I achieved as an athlete. At that time, I did not understand the idea of the person inside being bigger than all of that.

My job was part of my identity too, in the same way running had identified me. Take that away and who was I? Well, that's a good question to ask yourself now and again.

I grew up as an athlete and wanted from very early on to get into the field of sports medicine. When the time came in high school to begin to think seriously about college and a career, I started to explore the ways I could get into this particular field. I signed up to listen to a physical therapist speak at our career center at lunch one day and came home very excited.

I thought this might be the way. By the way she spoke about it, I could tell that she was inspired by her job, loved what she did, and made a good living doing it. I immediately called around to see if I could get a volunteer position at a clinic so I could really see if this was the career for me.

I later landed a part-time paid position as an aide in an outpatient physical therapy clinic and ended up working there until I graduated high school. By then, I knew this was the field I wanted to be in, but the challenge was going to be about getting accepted into physical therapy school, which at the time was very competitive.

I was turned down by UCSF and waitlisted by Samuel Merritt College, where I eventually was accepted and from which I graduated with my Master's in Physical Therapy. Before getting into college, though, I spent the hours waiting for replies and feeling heavy amounts of anxiety. I thought the worst about not getting into any school, not being good enough, and not ever succeeding in the field in which I wanted to work. I can see now that all that worrying was wasted time.

Once I started physical therapy school, I *loved* it much, much more than any school I'd been in before that. I loved learning about the body and all of its miraculous workings. We were taught the basics about the hands-on treatments that would later be the complete focus of my practice.

Only later did I realize how little they taught us in school. I loved the hands-on practice and I was told I was good at it, even as a student. During this time, I was lucky to have been doing one of my practical affiliations with a gentleman who was a teacher of a course called *Functional Orthopedics*.

I was able to sign up for the course he was teaching that year— a course that was usually reserved for licensed practitioners—as a student. What I learned that weekend catapulted me into the world of healing, introducing me to the idea that I could learn to help people heal in many different ways, one of the best being with my own hands.

I started to learn how to feel the muscle and connective tissue and how to release it when it was restricted. I would go on to take many more continuing education courses after graduation, and, along with having amazing and some not-so-amazing mentors, my ongoing education would be one of the ways I would learn how to facilitate healing in others. It would also be one of the ways I figured out how I wanted to practice, and how I did not want to practice.

Many courses I've taken are labeled as "traditional" physical therapy. Many of my favorites are labeled "alternative." Why have the alternative techniques and approaches been my favorite? Because they're holistic. They've been the way I've learned that we must treat the whole body, mind, and spirit of our patients before they will begin to really heal.

Can I help someone get better from their ankle sprain without treating their whole self? Probably. Will they come back for the pain in their middle back six months later because I forgot to look at the whole system? Hmm.

The alternative kinds of courses were reminding me of how I felt after a session with Robin, like real healing was happening. The kind of healing that fell into the category of finding your purpose in life and the answers to what makes you happy. How does that help your back pain? You'd be surprised.

In many cases, traditional physical therapy works well. We help people get stronger after a long hospitalization, we give them a program to rehabilitate their knee reconstruction, we teach them core exercises so that their back pain is lessened. Now, having over eighteen years of practice under my belt examining and speaking with so many different people, I'm realizing that I'm way more interested in a bigger picture of healing.

The physical body is the baby stuff. I believe this's what Robin was talking about when she told me that. It's the baby stuff, and it's also the door to the connection of body, mind, and spirit, because we feel through our body and its senses. What was missing in traditional approaches was being with and touching our patients, as well as helping them connect mind to body to spirit.

I now spend a lot of my time teaching people what it means to feel and how that'll help them heal. We work on body awareness and breathing. We work on listening to the body's signals and to the information we get from its tissues. It's too bad I didn't learn this stuff in school.

The two main avenues I've followed for learning and teaching healing have been craniosacral therapy and myofascial release. These are two approaches taught by different individuals in the physical therapy world.

My training in craniosacral therapy has been through the Up-ledger Institute, which is based in Florida, and I have learned the John F. Barnes Myofascial Release technique from John F. Barnes, who has treatment centers in Arizona and Pennsylvania.

I began to learn how to feel when I started doing this training. I was able to feel tight muscles, and then I was able to feel when bones were out of alignment. I started to feel the release of a fascial restriction under my hand.

Fascia—a tough connective tissue that travels from head to toe, three dimensionally, like a web in the body—can be restricted and bound down from trauma, inflammation or posture. In its healthy state, it's a system that contains and transports the fluid of our body. In a restricted state, it can put many pounds of excessive pressure on structures of the body, like nerves, muscles, blood vessels, and bones and organs, causing pain.

Myofascial release works to restore the fluidity of the tissue and the normal length and function of the tissue, which relieves pain and increases flexibility.

One of the phenomena I've been learning about is what happens to us in the connections of the mind and body when we go through trauma. What the myofascial release instructors teach is that the fascial tissue has memory. When the energy of the impact of a trauma enters the body, it can become lodged in the tissues, which can then hold that pent-up energy for months and years, causing that tissue to tighten and dehydrate over time.

The tissue holds a "memory" of the trauma. Myofascial release can address the tissue restrictions as well as help to release the stuck energy that is causing the restriction. This energy can be physical and emotional and most of the time is a combination of both.

For more information about this topic, you might be interested in picking up John's book, *Healing Ancient Wounds,* or the book by Bessel van der Kolk, MD, *The Body Keeps the Score.*

I started to be able to feel when I was anxious, nervous, fearful and lacking self-confidence. These emotions had physical feelings in my body, like tightness and pain. All of these things went together. My own healing made the space required for helping others to heal. I learned to ground and center my own body and mind. I learned to let go and relax so that I could soften and feel what was going on in someone else's body. I learned to notice my own thoughts and clear my mind so that I was able to feel anything at all. I started to love my job.

That's really something I've always said, that I love what I do, but at this point I began to love it because my worlds were melding together. The exploration of my own pain and restrictions, both physical and mental, and my ability to address and heal them was melding with my ability to hold a healing space for my client to do their healing work in.

This is what I'd heard and read about, but it hadn't really become a reality for me until then. My work began to be my play, and a different possibility for the way I was living came to be.

So *who I am is what I do* can now be said with a new feeling of confidence. I am a grounded and open presence who's conscious of an energy within her that serves her and all others she encounters. That energy is love, in case you were wondering.

I practice feeling it every day so that what I do for a living continues to be the best expression of that. I practice feeling it in all of the other areas of my life so that my moments, either alone or in connection with others, become an expression of it. Some moments are more challenging than others (such as this moment, while I listen to my children on this Sunday morning chasing each other through the house with some sort of homemade slingshot they've constructed out of sticks and rubber bands), but I enjoy the practice.

Ultimately, I've come to the conclusion that who I am isn't anything I do or any of the roles I play in life. I am love and joy. It would take me a while to get to that. In the next chapter, I break down some of the addictions I had to move through and detach from so I could get to the true me.

How can what you do be an expression of whom you truly are?

Use these pages to record your thoughts about the questions at the beginning and end of the chapter...

Addiction

What are you addicted to, good or bad?
I've written a lot about the addiction factor of Tae Kwon Do. Others have too. It's a mystery how many of us middle-aged mothers have talked about being addicted to a sport where we usually come home several times a week with a new bruise. The thing is, we also usually come home with a sense of achievement and a morsel of new confidence as well as a general feeling of awesomeness. Mystery solved. I enjoy being addicted to something that moves my life in a positive direction.

Journal entry November 29, 2006

Did some funny tweaker thing to my hip in class yesterday. All we did was kick yesterday, yikes! And watched board breaking. We will test for our green stripe Monday night!

Honestly, there is something totally cool about this sport. I'm so addicted. Never thought I could/would be. It was great to watch everyone and clap yesterday. And then when they were done, Jonathan's friend Dylan walked over and Jon says, "Congratulations!" It was so great! That part of me wishes he could have the audience. But there's a reason for everything. Looking forward also to getting our sparring gear, but that makes me nervous also. Jonathan can't wait. Not sure why. I'm pretty sure he just doesn't know his size... but really I guess that doesn't matter if he is paired with his size.

This was my realization about my addiction to exercise:

For true healing to occur, we have to feel and process the stuff of our lives. I'm talking about a bigger picture type of healing here, not just mending a cut or sprained ankle, or recovering from a head cold or surgery. That is physical healing. I'm talking about the kind of healing that's made up of forgiveness, and compassion, and expressing your deepest passionate self.

There are many ways that people numb themselves out when they either aren't capable or are afraid of feeling the feelings that need healing.

Some people are alcoholics, some people do drugs, some people won't stop talking, some won't get off the computer, some people overeat...I exercise. And sometimes I eat chocolate.

I started playing soccer as a pee wee and played through my sophomore year in college, all the while running as a way to condition myself for soccer. Then I started really running and ran the three marathons I mentioned previously. Six years ago, I started taking Tae Kwon Do lessons, and I am now three months from testing for my black belt. I'm addicted to exercise. And sugar.

But it's really the achievement that I'm addicted to.

I picked sports and achievement as my drug. It hit me this morning in the shower as I ruminated over Master Holloway's "take a Valium and do it again" comment.

From a really early age, I picked sports as my drug to either numb me or jazz me up when I was down. The focus of sports kept me alive; it was part of my identity, and my spirit soared there. So, it's not an illegal drug, but it's just as powerful and addictive. Is it a healthy drug? This's the dilemma in my mind today as I write.

Being high on exercise can help me perform when I need that crazy extra power and drive, i.e. board breaking or sparring. When I'm high on my drug and then I have to slow down and focus, I find doing so difficult. I'm tired, off balance, not breathing right, all of which are no help when you are performing Won-Hyo (a blue belt form) for the 86th time.

Can I make my drug work for me in all areas? Can I learn to focus my high so all the positive effects come together for a more peak performance? Probably. Is being high on this drug bad?

Today, with awareness, I'll say no. Although I've learned that you cannot selectively numb emotions.

"When you numb the pain, you also numb the joy." Brené Brown

We are our own worst judge, so I try to be aware of that and be gentle with myself. The part that's unhealthy is using exercise as an escape, to make me feel different because I don't want to feel the way I feel. Rather than just facing the fear or the feeling and moving through it, I like taking my "drug" because it makes me feel powerful and joyous again.

There are weeks when I lie awake at night waiting until the next day when I can get my fix, craving it, and not wanting to be where I am. But where I am is all I have, so the bad part is not recognizing life is in the moment and being okay with being present, even if I am sad, bored, angry, empty, or unhappy. Being addicted to elation is what I've been accused of. Isn't everyone? Aren't we all looking for the next happy moment?

What if every moment is perfect how it is, even the crappy ones? Would the idea be to just surf those waves whether you're gliding on top of them or whether they're crashing down on top of you? I will keep this drug for now, and break a few good boards in the meantime. Maybe a healthy passion is a positive addiction.

Journal entry October 5, 2006

Had Tae Kwon Do tonight—good class. We learned a lot tonight... but now I'm all jacked up from the workout...or maybe it was the dark chocolate M&M's? They asked us about sparring gear today too. Maybe for Christmas...

I was a soccer player from elementary school until my sophomore year of college. I was good. I loved soccer; it made me feel important. It kept me from joining the back parking lot crowd in high school. You know, the cigarette-smoking, class-ditching crowd? I cared more about staying in shape so I could perform on the field and for my team than I did about fitting into any other group of kids. Thank God.

I'm sure I was addicted to exercise even back then...it's what allowed me to feel like I belonged. The same question enters my mind now: "Is this a bad thing?"

When I was sixteen, my boyfriend at the time thought the way to teach someone to ski was to take them to the top of the mountain and make them go down. "Come on, I'll help you, don't worry," he said.

This was no beginner slope. I fell. A lot. I fell so badly at one point that the ski pole cord wrapped around my thumb and ripped it backward, leaving me with a limp digit. I made my way down the rest of the mountain foot by foot, trying to wipe the tears out of my eyes so I could see where I was going. My thumb hurt so badly that when I went in to use the bathroom, I could not button my jeans back up.

Fast forward to the doctor's office. Huge needle piercing my thumb joint. The kind that they do to numb you up just so they can examine the joint to see how badly the ligaments have been torn.

"Mom, I'm going to pass out," I cried. My whole body broke into a sweat, and I had to lie down on the examining table.

(And I later picked acupuncture as my main form of health care? Really?)

"We're going to have to put a cast on and hope it heals," said the doctor.

"You may have to have surgery if it doesn't heal properly," he finished.

A cast? I thought. I hadn't broken anything, for God's sake. Why were they putting a cast on me?

Any normal teenager would have been thrilled—a cast! Ooh, that'll be an attention-getter. I can have that cute boy in my science class sign it! Not me; I knew I wouldn't be able to play in the soccer game that weekend, and, remember, I was addicted. Plus, as a starting fullback on my varsity team, I didn't want to let my team down.

Fast forward once more to the following weekend's soccer match against our rival, Tamalpais High School. I shuffled into the line-up with the long sleeve of my jersey pulled down over my cast, hoping nobody would notice. Well, they noticed. "You can't play with a cast on!" The ref pointed at my arm.

"Miércoles!" I said, walking off the field with tears in my eyes. My good friend Grace taught me how to not really swear in Spanish, but sound like you are so it feels just as good.

I went home that day and mumbled to my mom, "Going out to the shed."

"Okay, honey," she replied, making herself busy in the kitchen.

I promptly found my mom's pruning shears in the tool shed and cut the cast off of my hand. Oh yeah, I did it, much to my mom's dismay. I happily played the next soccer game too, without a care about my mangled thumb.

Funny how I don't remember much more about that time, other than can you say, "grounded"? on Fast forward for the last time to about 1997 and my first job in a real orthopedic physical therapy setting, my second job ever. My thumb began to hurt so badly that I could no longer hold a pen to write my notes.

Ah, karma's a bitch, huh?

I found a brilliant hand surgeon who fixed me right up with a new thumb ligament, and I'm happy to say that my thumb is awesome. If only I'd listened to the doctor back then, though. Might have saved myself a little surgical PTSD.

As I write, I've been sending a chapter or two at a time to my mom (had to start with an easy critic). After she emails to tell me my writing is "just wonderful" and that "you should be so proud of yourself," I email back to ask what she thinks could be improved. My mom writes reports for a living and is a darn good writer and proofreader.

The last chapter I sent her was this one about being addicted to Tae Kwon Do. Her question was about pain. She wanted me to answer the question I asked in the beginning of this chapter out loud, and not leave it up to my readers to decide if I was a sadomasochist.

I was curious too. Was I really addicted to pain? To punching and kicking my way out of my troubles?

The day I wrote this chapter, my sister emailed me a blog link about writing. It was fantastic. The author included a quote that answered my question brilliantly:

"We must all suffer one of two things: the pain of discipline or the pain of regret and disappointment." Jim Rohn

I'll take door number one, Alex. Way easier. But occasionally, I might get kicked in the head.

In his blog, Chris Guillebeau says, "Make your art your obsession. Fall in love with it. Experience withdrawal symptoms when you don't give it your attention."

Yes, I think this includes martial arts. I've been there and done that. Now that someone else says it's okay, I think I'll just love being addicted. Join me?

Follow me into the next chapter as I move through my fears, embrace the passions—addicted or not—and then get a tattoo.

What addictions have become your passion? How do you feel when you are wrapped up in them?

Use these pages to record your thoughts about the questions at the beginning and end of this chapter...

Fear, Freedom and Tattoos

What holds you back from doing what you want to do? If you could overcome the fear and do that one thing, how would it feel?

My thirty-ninth birthday year fell in 2007. It was all about breaking out and being free. It was about becoming more of myself and making my own choices. This was the year I decided to get a tattoo.

"Let the world know you as you are, not as you think you should be, because sooner or later, if you are posing, you will forget the pose, and then where are you?" Fanny Brice

"One of the greatest feelings in life is the conviction that you have lived the life you wanted to live - with the rough and the smooth, the good and the bad - but yours, shaped by your own choices, and not someone else's." Michael Ignatieff

Journal entry February 17, 2007, two days after my thirty-ninth birthday

I did it. I got my dragonfly tattoo on my right back above my hip. My best friend Shelly and I celebrated our thirty-ninth birthdays with tattoos and piercings (she got the belly button pierce). Can you say "midlife crisis?" I cried in the car on the way home. They were relief tears. Tears of freedom, which is what the dragonfly symbolizes to me.

Listen carefully, children: the tattoo hurt like hell. It hurt so bad that when I was done, I realized I had sweat completely through my pink button-down shirt. It hurt so bad that I started to feel sick and had to make the tattoo artist stop and let me lie down.

Thoughts of my worst nightmare roamed in my head...a one-winged dragonfly. But after a few minutes, the nausea passed, she finished, and I was okay. Phew! My friend Shelly looked at me and said, "Are you okay?" Evidently I was pale.

"I'm good," I said, not so convincingly.

Shelly and I drove to my place, had some 2003 Beringer Shiraz with dark chocolate truffles, and lifted our shirts for each other so we could inspect the results of our insanity.

"Let me see!" I said. We talked and laughed, and I felt good. James Brown style.

I felt good because I did something I'd always wanted to do, without asking permission. Maybe part of it was me wanting to say, "Screw you, I'm going to do this anyway."

But honestly it felt more like, "My path, my body, my passion; I will choose, and I hope you love me anyway." In that moment, I was 39 years old, with a husband, two kids, and a career, and I'd made a choice for myself, without anyone else's approval. That decision broke me free from a fear inside of me about doing or saying something that might make someone else mad.

This was important. And really scary. What was I afraid of? Turns out I should've been afraid of it hurting like hell. But I was truly afraid of rejection. Of getting in trouble. Of being a bad girl. Of feeling unworthy and unlovable. All deep childhood wounds.

Thoughts of divorce went through my head. My husband (now my ex) deserved way more credit than that, yet inside of me, that's what was going on. I was making a permanent change that someone else didn't approve of. I think this was worse than getting kicked in the head. That would come later.

To me, fear means False Evidence Appearing Real.

"Fears are educated into us, and can if we wish, be educated out."
Karl Augustus Menninger

"A ship is safe in harbor, but that's not what ships are for."
William Shedd

When I say, "I'm afraid to," what does that mean? Maybe that there is some outcome I'm expecting that would be bad. That the outcome would be injurious to me in some way either psychologically or physically. Or that the outcome would just make me look bad, assuming I care what other people think.

That's the real problem, isn't it? We all care about what other people think of us, to the point of being afraid to be ourselves. To the point of letting others choose for us.

If the label "fear" didn't exist, then fear would exist only as a feeling inside of me. Meaning that when I become afraid, I feel my heart beating very fast, my skin sweating, my chest tightening, or my stomach turning.

It's interesting to me that one response to fear can be an intuitive protective mechanism, like the fight-or-flight response, that allows you to know when a situation is dangerous. Another response can be feeling paralyzed, squelching your full creative self-expression.

The kind of fear that blocks us; makes us feel constrained, hopeless, and frustrated; and leaves us feeling defeated and less than ourselves is the type of fear to act on in spite of our reaction. The kind that my entire life has been about overcoming.

The feeling of moving into and through this type of fear is liberating. The thoughts are, *I did it, I survived, it's about time, and I can do anything.* These thoughts have a different quality about them inside of the body. They are the adrenaline rush, beating heart, tingling, smiling, shining-out-on-the-world type of feelings. They attract others. They are breathless, exhilarating, and ultimately addictive, I think. You know, bungee-jumping, race-car-driving addictive. That's one end of the spectrum, anyway.

Most of us are so stuck in fear that we can't even imagine that end of the spectrum. Fear becomes paralyzing for us. Instead of living fiercely alive, we're trapped, thinking we're supposed to suffer, thinking that everyone else gets to run our show. Instead of knowing we are meant for joy and love, we think we deserve the suffering. We live like that's our reality. The truth is that it's all in our little heads.

Discipline the mind! I hear.

Meanwhile, our bodies constrict in fear, and we become smaller and tighter. It hurts. We're afraid to say it, to speak it out loud. We have no voice.

I lost my voice somewhere very early along the line. Afraid that what I had to say wasn't good enough. Afraid to make a fool of myself. Afraid that nobody would care about my story. Afraid to act. Afraid to be bad.

But my story is your story, and I have a voice. My voice, since it is also yours, might be the way of healing for you and for me. My voice counts. It's important. And none of those thoughts even matter without action. So what do I have to lose by taking one step closer to my dream, even if I am afraid?

Journal entry February 17, 2007

Had a great Tae Kwon Do class this morning; my calf did fine with a slight strain feeling. Found out that we will test for our green belt on Saturday! Can't wait! It will be a great end to a long week coming up. I think he'll be okay with the tattoo. He's still upset. Called Mom on the way home from class to tell her...she was proud of me.

I remember the fear I had during two different Tae Kwon Do tournaments when it was time to spar. During the first, I was a blue belt, and because there was no other competition in my rank category, they paired me with a red belt/black stripe. I agreed in terror.

The waiting period before the match was so long, and I'd worked myself up so much, that by the time we were ready to go, I could feel the power draining out of my legs.

I'm not really sure where it went, but it was not where I'd hoped. I lost the match but managed to score a few points against someone a whole belt rank higher, so I was proud of myself for trying. I fought in spite of my fear and survived, feeling better than before I started. I will describe this match and a bunch more about sparring a bit more in detail later.

In the second match a year or so later, there were about four people in my category to spar against. I could feel the fear and anxiety creeping back in and had decided not to spar at all that day. I was gently coaxed out of the bleachers by Master M, and I let her talk me into trying it.

The waiting period during this tournament was torturously long, and I decided I'd have to do this waiting differently than before if I wanted any chance of fighting well. So this time I decided to lie down in the gym while we were waiting, tune the sounds and lights out, and rest. I tried to clear my mind and pull myself out of my fear head. I went on to win my first and second matches of the day and to score a gold medal for sparring.

There's an obvious difference in my preparation technique between the two episodes, and it was all mental. In both cases, I was equally prepared physically. In the second, I was smart, calm, and grounded mentally.

Fear is first conquered in the mind and then with the body in action. This kind of fear is a type of performance anxiety. I'm learning that I can use that fear energy that's in me and turn it into energy used *for* me. This has taken a lot of practice.

I also struggle with another kind of fear that leaves me small and quiet: the fear of asking for what I want (because it might make someone mad). The feeling inside me when my father would be angry or disappointed with something I'd done was too much to bear as a child. I went into survival mode and just shut down and shut up.

That feeling stuck with me into adulthood as I began having

to deal with male authority figures in my life. Teachers, doctors, and some boyfriends would trigger the feeling, and I would always lose out, shriveling back into the corner without any response to defend myself.

It continued with my husband at the time, and almost every time I was afraid of asking for something, the thought, instead of being expressed, just stayed in my head, stuffed into some hole inside me that was used to being a container for those unspoken desires. Until that container got too full and couldn't hold any more. I was afraid he would be angry or disagree or that he'd think I was stupid.

That felt familiar.

Overcoming this kind of fear, something I now call purpose-driven fear, of authentically communicating my truth with others, has been a huge healing event in my life. More on fear, finding my voice, and healing later on. But first, a chapter about friendship and how that moved me through on the worst days.

How would it feel to be afraid and act anyway? In what instances in your life have you been able to overcome fear and move through? In what instances do you still feel stuck?

Use these pages to record your thoughts about the questions at the beginning and end of this chapter...

Friends

W<i>hat does friendship mean to you?</i>
I've been lucky to have a few best friends in my life, and during these years of growth, healing, and transformation, I have been lucky to have one or two hang around to see the outcome of what had to appear as totally chaotic from the outside. There've been times I haven't been so great to be around. I appreciate my friends and feel they have saved me from insanity some days.

My friend Shelly and I have known each other for more than fifteen years. She's been a special friend to me. We've been in each other's weddings, supported each other's pregnancies, watched our kids grow together, listened to each other's stories, and laughed and cried together. She has been one of the few people in my life that has put up with my shit without judging me.

I called Shelly in tears one day. It was the middle of her work day.

"It's George," I said. "She won't get up."

Our black lab mutt was fourteen years old, and that day, when the kids and I had come home with our usual chaotically loud entrance, our usual greeting committee was not there.

"Jon, can you go down and check on George for me, buddy?" I asked, thinking it was just taking her a bit longer to get up the stairs on those arthritic hips.

A few minutes later, when I heard Jonathan's voice hollering up at me from the basement, I knew.

"Mom! She won't get up!" Danielle and I ran downstairs together and found Jonathan kneeling next to George. She looked up at us but didn't budge, no tail wag, nothing.

"Come on Georgie!" the kids pleaded. "Let's go, come on!"

Still no movement. We brought a bowl of water and food down to her to see if she was interested, but no luck. That night, we carried her upstairs and helped her onto a blanket to sleep. My heart was breaking.

"I don't think I can do this by myself," I cried to my friend on the phone the next day, explaining that my husband was on a business trip.

"I'm on my way over," Shelly said, and I sat next to my sweet dog with her chin on my leg and stroked her velvety ears until she got there. We carried George to the car and brought her to the vet together. We sat on the floor of the examining room with George and cried together, and it was the suckiest thing I have ever done, watching the remaining life drain from my puppy's eyes that watched mine until the last moment.

I will always remember Shelly for what she did for me that day. For being willing to drop everything and show up to be by my side for something so sad. She just sat with me and cried and didn't say a word. That's all I needed. I just didn't want to be alone. Knowing I have a friend like her helps me not be afraid. Of anything, really. Together, we can face anything. Together, we are stronger, and the pain is less.

"When we honestly ask which persons in our lives mean the most to us, we often find that it is those who, instead of giving much advice, solutions, or cures, have chosen rather to share our pain and touch our wounds with a gentle and tender hand. The friend who can be silent with us in a moment of despair or confusion, who can stay with us in an hour of grief and bereavement, who can tolerate not-knowing, not-curing, not-healing, and face with us the reality of our powerlessness...makes it clear that whatever happens in the external world, being present to each other is what really matters." Henri F. M. Nouwen

There've been many an hour that I've sat with my girlfriends and worked life out in those moments together. Through talking, venting, explaining, listening, crying, and laughing (until our faces hurt), I swear we have it *all* worked out. I remember a weekend last year that I spent with my friends Shelly and Jill. The three of us drove down to the Outer Banks to celebrate Shelly's new beach house and break it in, girl-style.

I was contemplating a huge career shift in those months, and something pulled inside of me. The girls and I took our glasses of sangria down to the little dock behind the house. The wood was warm under my bare feet.

It was nice enough that April to sport tank tops. "I'm thinking of partnering with a group of therapists to form a larger wellness center," I said. I shared the details of pros and cons to see if they had some ideas or suggestions for me.

The thing about good friends is you can't really hide anything from them; they know you too well. That is a blessing. I started talking to Jill about wanting to teach Tae Kwon Do and how I felt inside of me that I was meant to do it.

I had to stop talking, cover my face (so they wouldn't see it scrunch up in a cry), and lie down on the dock with my feet dangling over the edge as the tears streamed down my face.

Sometimes you don't know the answer to your dilemma until the words fly out of your mouth and the tears come falling down. I didn't want to be a business partner and give up the life balance I'd worked so hard for. The timing wasn't right.

I was feeling and following my Tae Kwon Do passion, and that had made me so happy. And I still doubted it. I thought that success meant bigger, better, and more.

But true success means being happy, joyful, calm, and able to help others. It means following your passion. It means your work is your play. It has the meaning you give it, not what other people think it means.

I've learned to trust the emotions, so I immediately sent my good friend Phil, who was also a prospective business partner, an email. I let him know how I was feeling and then closed my eyes and crossed my fingers that he wouldn't hate me.

At that point in time, we'd already had meetings that included the four of us who would partner together and had looked at possible real estate for our venture. We had brainstormed parts of a business plan and discussed everyone's role in it.

Following my gut and then sending the email sucked. I worried that I was burning bridges with people I really respected and wanted to keep as friends.

I laughed out loud when I quickly received an email back from Phil that said: "I met with Rosine" (his psychic) "today and she let me know that the business venture wasn't the right timing for me."

So he knew before I could tell him. On top of knowing already, he was the kind, gracious, amazing friend he's always been and let me know that everything was okay. No, he didn't hate me. Love you, Phil. Phil even came to try Tae Kwon Do with me one day!

The friends I've had in my life are amazing. Some old, some new, some good, some bad, some unexpected. They've made me feel worthy by being interested in me and my stories and by wanting to spend time with me.

Some friends have given me the opportunity to grow as a person, to realize mistakes, to be bigger and better. Some have been a mirror. Some have refused to put up with me and walked away. Some have made me squirm, and others have made me dance.

I'm lucky enough to be able to say that my sister has been one of my best friends my whole life. We've been through the same childhood together and survived better for having each other. We enjoy spending time together, laughing and talking together. We can sit with each other in silence and feel completely comfortable together this way too.

Being able to sit in silence with someone is an interesting test of true friendship and comfortable connection. We pass that test. We can relax together.

My sister graduated with her master's degree in marriage and family counseling. Having a sister who can analyze and provide perspective about our family is priceless. The way she is able to listen and guide during the times I'm at my very worst is better than having my own private therapist, because it is having one who has loved me my whole life.

It's the friends who love without judging that I value the most. The ones who can be themselves and let me do the same, while realizing that it won't always be cozy and not caring. And showing up again.

The friends who will talk about life, death, sex, and Tae Kwon Do in the same conversation without missing a beat—those are the ones. The ones who make you laugh, who laugh at you and with you, and who laugh just to hear themselves laugh. Yeah, those friends...they lift me up. The friends who demand that I follow my intuition and support my healing process are special. They hold me accountable.

I lost a good friend over a weird, meaningless argument one year. She had not responded to an invitation I sent for my son's birthday party, so I emailed to see if her son would attend. She said yes. When she and her husband arrived with their son and older daughter, I was a little surprised.

The party was at a local bowling alley, and this was the first year Jonathan decided only boys were allowed (except his sister). My friend did not know that of course, but since she hadn't bothered to respond to my invitation, I was already a little mad.

"Can she stay and help with the party?" she asked. I came up with some lame story about feeling bad that I didn't have any extra goodie bags to soften the blow of my "no." My friend grabbed her daughter's hand and stormed out of the bowling alley, leaving her husband behind with their son.

I tried to call her cell phone immediately to tell her I was sorry and that of course her daughter could stay and help. "Can you please call her and tell her to answer her phone?" I pleaded with her husband. "I'll try," he said.

That wasn't going to work either. I made several attempts over many months to reconcile through emails, phone calls, and a letter.

We even met in person to talk it out, and at one point I thought we might be okay.

We were never friends after that. Losing a girlfriend like this hurt in a way that I hadn't experienced before. It was different from any love interest I'd ever had. It was harder for some reason.

I wanted her to understand what she did wrong. I wanted to be right, and I wasn't willing to not be right, to lose face. I thought I was apologizing, but I realized later that I wasn't really. I just wanted to make up, for everything to be okay, so that I didn't have "failed friendship" on my resumé.

The hardest part about losing this friend was that the two of us were a part of a five-some of friends that regularly spent time together, and quite often with our husbands. We valued this group of friends a lot and other people lost out because of our stupid fight.

When I think about it now, I still regret the loss, but after so many attempts at contacting her, I feel like my welcome is completely worn out and that at least I don't have to regret never trying. I put this story in the "life is weird" pile. I had to grow up a little after that one. I wasn't in kindergarten anymore, and hurt feelings had a different cost now than they used to. I would pick my battles more carefully in the future.

One thing I've learned is that it's never too late to make a friend. You only have to be authentic and willing and give it some energy. If people would only be willing to open their hearts for each other, to be curious about the adventure of life, including the people who show up on your doorstep, amazing things could happen.

"Connection is why we are on the planet." Brené Brown

The awareness I gained through my friendships woke me up. Awareness became a central theme of my healing journey. In the next chapter, I talk about this practice and how it became the foundation of everything moving forward.

Who are the people in your tribe and why?

Use these pages to record your thoughts about the questions at the beginning and end of this chapter...

Staying Here in Now

I n the moments of your day, where are you?

Present moment awareness is one of the secrets to a life lived with joy and passion. Add in detaching from the outcome (not judging things), gratitude, and taking action in the direction of your dreams, and you have the recipe for a small miracle.

Green Belt Exam Essay February 24, 2007

I suppose I could write about many different things that have had my attention since our last test. Being able to break a board with my jumping back kick without ever having practiced that move before was a thrill. Watching my six-year-old son succeed at doing that was even better.

Starting to spar has been interesting. Learning to get used to a mouth guard and being able to speak with it in is a talent in and of itself. Sparring with partners twice as big and tall as I am—as well as those twice as small—has been a lesson in adaptability. Learning that the act of sparring will make you lose your breath faster than running a 5K race was an eye-opener. Feeling my body get better at it has been rewarding.

However, something else I have been working on since the green stripe has felt much more essay-worthy. It has to do with the saying by Master Holloway, "Discipline the mind, the body will follow." One hears and reads about this idea a lot. The idea that discipline of the mind comes first, and then the rest will be a piece of cake. Yet many of us strive for physical fitness as our first priority, leaving mental clarity for if or when we have time. And who ever has the time?

What many of us don't realize until we try it is that healing and freeing the mind, being in our moments, meditating, or whatever other way you like to describe it, is the path to things like peak physical performance and happiness, simply enough. For some, it is easy enough to sit in meditation every day and learn to practice this ancient art until we are still and peaceful and can actually access stillness on demand. Most of the rest of us, it seems, need serious help in the relaxation department, with a still and peaceful mind sounding like something only monks get to experience.

The key is to get help. Maybe you start with yoga. Maybe you need to work with someone who can teach you meditation or deep breathing. Maybe acupuncture, or possibly another kind of therapy, works for you. After dabbling with many of the above-mentioned practices, I started trying acupuncture, which at first was meant to help with a common cold. Now, I experience deep relaxation and peace that carries on past my session through my workday and my week.

Robin, my acupuncturist, has taught me what it means and how it feels to be in the moment, and how that frees both the mind and the body. I feel strength not only in my muscles and my immune system, but also in my mind and emotions. I am lighter.

So, as I get closer to a full split stretch, noticing that my 38-year-old hips hurt less, and as I look at the clock and realize I have been sparring with a six-foot-three-inch-tall man for over two minutes and feel like I could keep going, I realize that my physical conditioning is only partly the reason I have achieved these things. The more fascinating and inspiring reason is that I can relax in the moment with a freer mind, and that this lightness is what allows my joints to move and my heart to pump more effectively. This is a cool thing.

For this essay, I reviewed two articles. The first article, "Tae Kwon Do And The Brain," from Taekwondo Times magazine, explains how the brain, through things like breath awareness and meditation, helps us to gain confidence, let go of anxieties, and achieve peak performance. The authors describe the form as a moving meditation that uses concentration and mindfulness to help us focus. The effects can last even after a session. In a grander sense, they describe the benefits as far-reaching as being able to achieve selflessness and peace, which would have positive effects for the world.

The article "Train Your Brain" from Runner's World magazine describes how scientists are disproving an old theory about muscle fatigue. They say that the idea that you fatigue due to lactic acid build-up or a depletion of muscle glycogen is false. And they are starting to prove that the brain is in control and that you can train yourself to fatigue more slowly.

The new theory, called the central governor theory, tells us that you can beat muscle fatigue by doing race- or competition-specific training, proving to your brain that you can do the work. When the performance day comes, your brain should respond by delaying the signals to your muscles that would have otherwise caused an earlier fatigue. This might put an end to the old excuses like "I just ran out of energy" or "I just didn't have anything left."

Journal entry February 24, 2007

Today we did our green belt test...I guess this is perfect with St. Patrick's Day coming! I was surprised that we didn't do board breaking...they asked us to do the bag instead, and I was afraid of messing up my leg again, so I asked if I could pass. It was no problem, but I was disappointed. It would have been fun to try it with everyone there. Our family, too. It was nice to have them all there. Dani seemed to like to watch. I have felt anxious today, though. Restless. I went for a short run, and my calf seemed to hold okay. I almost did a full split today. Jonathan did thirty kicks on the bag!

Journal entry March 2007:

Last night we went to an extra TKD class at 6:15 p.m. It was great, and green was the top color! Jonathan ran to be at the end and head of the class, and he wasn't giving it up for anything. He said "Cha Rutt" (attention) and "Kyung Yet" (bow) just great.

During these last several years, I began a reading binge that started with a little movie someone emailed to me called *The Secret*. The ideas of the power of positive thinking and the law of attraction had always sparked my interest. A lot.

I wanted to read anything I could get my hands on about it. Some of the books that completely changed the way I thought about my thinking and my life were:

The Secret by Rhonda Byrne
Wherever You Go There You Are by John Kabot-Zinn
A New Earth by Eckhart Tolle
True Meditation by Adyashanti
Spiritual Liberation by Michael Bernard Beckwith
Excuses Begone by Dr. Wayne Dyer (who also made a little movie you should watch called *The Shift)*
The Invitation by Oriah Mountain Dreamer
Way of the Peaceful Warrior by Dan Millman
Healing Ancient Wounds (mentioned earlier) by John F. Barnes
The Power by Rhonda Byrne
The Art of Effortless Living by Ingrid Bacci, Ph.D.
Full Body Presence by Suzanne Scurlock-Durana

I found myself nodding my head as I read these books. I took notes. I practiced what they preached. I taught the ideas to my clients. They seemed important, especially if you wanted a life of joy.

Ultimately, the reason they sounded good was because I felt something was missing from my life. I started asking myself questions. Was I happy? Why did I worry so much? Why couldn't I just enjoy the moment? What was this feeling that I had in my chest that made me feel like I couldn't breathe?

Journal entry August 10, 2007

Yesterday in Tae Kwon Do class, I came very close to a full split stretch. This is something I really never believed my hips would achieve. As I gradually eased myself closer to the floor, I was shocked at the improvement, remembering that the same position just five days earlier did not yield the same results.

I can feel less surprised I suppose if I look at the effort, a year and a half worth, that I have made toward this goal. If I look at it that way, I might wonder what took me so long. I'd rather look at it over my lifetime of inflexibility, thirty-nine years' worth, and marvel at the advancement in just one and a half years of focus.

We can do great things with our bodies, achieve great changes, enjoy great fitness. We only need to mix effort and determination and point them at a goal. The body should comply. I suppose a split stretch was just never a goal before now. So the realization that we only need to set our goals and move toward them in order to achieve them is exciting. It means we can do anything. This we should teach our children.

Something else I will teach my kids is that we give life its meaning. So, when you begin to ask yourself, *What is the purpose of all of this?*, just know that you get to choose. (Seriously, how cool is that?)

The real questions should be:

> What lights my fire?
> What really turns me on?
> What gets me excited/motivated/inspired?

Add a cup of enthusiasm and a dash of determination to that passion, and you will never run out of purpose or meaning in your life. When you combine passion with present moment awareness, you begin to have a life that is full and rich and miraculous.

Funny part is, you already had that life. You just needed to do some fine-tuning of the lenses that you were wearing. Passion combined with awareness, coming from a place of gratitude—that's the recipe. It requires practice.

"Discipline the mind, the body will follow," Master John L. Holloway

The discipline of staying in the now and being the observer of your thoughts so you can tweak them when necessary is powerful. And then pay attention to the outcome of those tweaks. In this scenario, discipline gives you freedom—the freedom to choose your response. To change your thoughts.

Journal entry November 7, 2007
I felt like I had to remember the day of the Gentle East Captain's Cup Challenge. This day was one of my best. In the moment and saturated. So proud. So supported. I think I would do this again.

Blue Belt Essay December 1, 2007
Since our last exam, I had the pleasure and excitement of being able to participate in my first Tae Kwon Do tournament. I do not remember the last time I was so excited and nervous about competing in anything since maybe college soccer.

The event day was probably one of the most enjoyable and memorable days I've had with my family and one when I was most proud, of myself and of my son. To be able to participate in such an event with my son was a total joy.

We cheered each other on through each event with anticipation and hope for the gold. My son amazed me with his determination and fearlessness and made me proud with his display of good sportsmanship. I was thrilled to listen to my mom tell me afterward how he coached me during my sparring match and how he would shout out the number every time I scored a point. I was honored when he asked me to be his coach.

The first event that day was forms. My son competed in the second group according to age category. I stood and watched him and thought through each move of his form as he performed it for the judges. When he told me, "I had power and rhythm, Mom, that's why I won," he really nailed it. What a total thrill to see him win that event. A bit later, when I also nailed the form called Yul-Guk for the gold, I thought that we could have gone home at that point. How much better could this day have started out?

The next two events brought some bronze medals for Jonathan, and, I think even more than the medals, the feeling that putting out his best effort and experiencing all the things that a competition is about was worth its weight in gold. As a mom, I wished that all three medals were gold, but I also found great joy in watching him fight his best fight no matter what place he finished. I hoped that he would figure out by himself that sometimes it really is the fun of competing that counts, no matter the prize.

Meanwhile, my own competitive nature started to come through after winning silver in board breaking. Managing to break only one of my two boards and matched up against a woman who set up four stations and broke three, I began to wonder why I hadn't planned something more difficult. Now, this is after failing to break my 360-degree back kick that I had succeeded in breaking only days before in practice. Something more difficult? Was I insane? Truth is, I think this stuff is addictive. I should be thrilled that I broke even one of the boards, considering the amount of performance anxiety I was feeling. So, next time my test will be to master the breaking with the anxiety, to be able to channel the adrenaline; that is the key!

This issue hit home during the sparring event as well, when I felt my breath rattling harshly and uncontrollably in my throat. I was able somehow to use that crazy energy in my favor this time and managed to score three points.

Winning a gold in sparring was just plain fun. Never in a million years did I think I would be fully suited up and fighting against another almost-forty-year-old mom. Thank goodness there are other crazy people out there to spar against.

I also learned that it is possible to be in a gym full of people, with all kinds of noise and chaos going on around you, including your own son shouting at the top of his lungs, "You got one, Mom, you got one, now two, Mom, two!" and not hear anything but your own breath in your throat. It was like those shots in the movies when they cut out all the motion and all you see are the drops of sweat flying off the guy. Cool. But weird, too. Nothing I ever thought I would be experiencing.

At the end of the day, I was spent but smiling. I hope we get to do that again. I love Tae Kwon Do!

Red Stripe Essay April 26, 2008

I'm sitting and stretching, waiting for the class before me to finish so I can start mine. I'm watching the class, watching Jonathan and Danielle help Master Holloway show the beginner class how to do a low block. I am half here, watching but also thinking, not about what I'm watching but about a hundred other things that are occupying my mind.

Worrying about my new business, about schedules, about my sister who is depressed, about my patient who is going in for surgery. I'm physically here in the gym waiting for Tae Kwon Do to start but miles away in my mind, with all the worries and planning and stuff that is making me think it's all so important.

Now class begins, line up, feet together, my body knows what to do. I am here. I feel my feet touch, my hands press to my thighs, my body bend at the waist to bow. Finally, class begins, and I can be here, now.

The floor vibrates into my feet as I sense the movement of the students next to me through the bouncy floor. Jumping jacks, stretches, punches, kicks, and I start to feel the sweat around my face. My familiar aches work themselves out. Combinations, fundamental moves, my form…and I feel myself focus. I'm only here and now, and nothing else matters. Focus and freedom.

I was talking with a friend of mine the other day about being in the moment. We were talking about things that keep us in the moment and things we do when we're so far out of the moment, it's scary.

I am noticing all the times when my thinking takes over. The thinking is mostly worry about the future, or remembering some past moment. When I do this, I'm not paying attention to the only moment that really matters, which is the one I am in now.

I have been practicing this lately, this being in the moment. It makes everything interesting. I feel more alive to what is happening around me: people, nature, everything. It also wipes away any worry about the past or future, when I can get myself into the now.

I have found it a waste of time to worry about something that hasn't happened yet and another waste of time to worry about something that has already happened. Freedom. Slowing down, paying attention, with relaxed focus on the thing that is in front of you.

All of this seems like a miracle, seeing as I have been conditioned from an early age to worry. I somehow learned to worry about everything, like my worrying, if fierce enough, would produce some result. Well, I will tell you the result it brings: anxiety.

Present moment awareness is a practice, a discipline. The practice is catching yourself in your daily moments when over-thinking is taking over and then coming back into your center, into the now, with a clear, quiet focus. Negative thoughts have this way of sucking you in, and being self-perpetuating. Breaking out of that trance and into the now is the practice.

It's worth the effort.

When I'm in class, I'm in the moment, and it's beautiful, almost effortless. There are moments of distraction, like when I catch one of my kids misbehaving, but in general I can stay focused because I have to pay attention to what my body is doing.

If I don't, there's a consequence that has a way of slapping me in the face, and in Tae Kwon Do, that's sometimes literal. I used to call my running practice my meditation time. When I learned about the idea of the mind chatter, I realized that most of my meditative runs had been lost in thoughts, some good and some bad.

Since then, when I've tried to focus on the moments of the run itself, I have struggled to stay there, always seeming to drift back into thinking about something other than what I'm doing. It was easy to be distracted, because running is rhythmical and repetitive, and I seem to be able to run without really paying attention to the act of it.

With Tae Kwon Do, it's more difficult to be distracted and still practice. It requires the mind and the body to focus at once, and that's what I enjoy most about it.

There's power in the present moment when you are aware inside of it. That power has to do with a peace, freedom, creativity, calm, and stillness out of which anything can happen. If we can break out of the prison of our minds and live inside that stillness, we can achieve anything.

Sometimes at the end of class, after we line up and you ask us to close our eyes, the quiet envelops the room and my ears almost ring from the all-of-a-sudden silence. It's that rare moment when nobody is coughing or clearing their throat, there are no crying toddlers in the hallway, and the playground behind us is empty.

That quiet is rare and welcome to my soul. It demands presence, awareness. It makes me smile, with eyes still closed, because I know how many people are in the room, some having just sparred their brains out or kicked the crap out of the bags, students waiting, parents waiting for students.

All are silent for that sweet moment when there's nothing else but the space to notice it. I realize in that moment how my life lacks those quiet spaces. I'm so used to the noise of life, the voices, the sounds that constantly bombard us, numbing us up a little, distracting us from ourselves. My tolerance has diminished.

I don't often turn on the radio in the car anymore. Funny how the kids never ask me to. Maybe they enjoy those quiet spaces too. I feel like the older I get, the more I need the quiet to feel what is going on inside of me, to realize the important stuff, to stop myself from just keeping busy, to slow down, to breathe.

I practice using silence to clear my mind and notice what tapes try to play themselves in my head. Without judging, I clear my thoughts again and try to drop into my body instead. As I feel my body, with its aches or pains, feeling light or heavy, tight or loose, I'm grateful for it and for all the awesome things it can do. Please, just one more minute of sweet silence to nourish my soul.

In the next chapter, I take my awareness and put it into practice inside of the most difficult moments with my family. It always seems like the people who know you the best trigger you the most.

How would it feel to just be here, now? Can you pay attention to one thing at a time?

Use these pages to record your thoughts about the questions at the beginning and end of this chapter...

Family Effort and More Life

W*hat has "family" meant in your life?*
Part of my healing was being able to redefine what family meant. I wanted a team, to support each other, to win and lose together, and to rely on. I didn't realize how much work it was to keep a good family team together.

For eight short but sweet months, I had my whole family practicing Tae Kwon Do together on Saturday mornings. It didn't last for very long, but I treasure having that time when we shared the practice. Very recently, my daughter re-enrolled. I'm not going to hold my breath. Just going to enjoy being there with both my kids for as long as I get.

I know the influence of Tae Kwon Do goes well beyond the positives of an after-school activity. As the kids develop their own passions in life, I want to be around to encourage their involvement and excitement. For now, we can share one or two of those passions and enjoy the feeling of knowing we have someone to talk to about it.

Journal entry December 1, 2007

Today, my whole family did their Tae Kwon Do test together! Danielle and her dad got their yellow belts. Danielle was awesome! So was Daddy! Jonathan and I got our blue belts. Jonathan broke his board with a back kick. And I broke two boards with an axe kick. It felt so cool to break two boards. I was so proud, being there with my whole family. I love this stuff and am totally addicted. I hope I can teach some more again.

Danielle drew an awesome picture of herself doing Tae Kwon Do for her back-to-school night project. A nice L-stance double fore-arm block in the big, blue gym! I was so thrilled to see this picture that she chose to draw on her own, knowing that she was proud to be a martial artist!

Recently, Danielle and I were sitting together, reading our books while we waited for Jonathan's baseball game to start. Without taking her eyes away from the page, she asked, "Mom, what is an ashtray?"

Wow. So I guess no matter what happens, I'll at least know I did one thing right.

I've tried as a parent to do everything right, knowing I won't. Knowing that it won't really matter how hard I try, because there will be some little thing I say or do that will screw up my kid. But I continue to try.

Getting them involved in activities they enjoy, where they learn success and failure, passion, joy, and connection, would be the one thing I would like to do right, besides having them never smoke a cigarette.

Being involved in soccer saved me as a teenager. I needed saving. Maybe my kids won't need saving as much. Maybe I'm delusional.

The other thing I would like to do right is teach them how to feel and know it's natural and good to feel all the stuff of their lives. That feeling now will save them so much grief later.

I think they do feel everything, and it's the reaction of the adults around them that shapes what they think and how they express their feelings from there on out.

It's okay to cry. That's been repeated now so many times by so many different people that it has lost its mojo. It really is okay to cry, to show you are sad, to be sad with others, until you feel like the emotion is fully released. It's not only okay, it's necessary to feel those feelings if you want to have a life of joy and passion. We must clear out the sadness and the anger so that we can make room for something else bigger and better.

I want my kids to giggle and never forget how.

I've learned an incredible lesson by having a family. I have peeps. We are a team. We make a unit that has the option of being loving, strong, and supportive and can take on the world to do good. I never had that feeling as a kid.

My parents divorced when I was eight (my daughter's current age at the time of this writing). I've had two step-fathers and one step-mother since then. Instead of strengthening the team, I worried about which house I would have to go to on what weekend or holiday and whether one of my parents was upset that we were with the other instead of them. My parents were doing the best they could with what they had. I just did not ever have the idea of a strong, supportive family unit that empowered each other.

The paragraph you're now reading is a result of over-thinking, re-reading, and worrying about my mom. It's okay, Mom, and I'm not just writing this for you. I'm writing it for me too, to remind myself that part of who I am is where I came from, and that's a great thing.

I'm happy being me and feel grateful for all of it. The hard parts shaped me, taught me, gave me choices, and ultimately helped me be me. What I worried about when I re-read the paragraph above was that my parents (mostly my mom) would think that because I wrote it, they failed somehow.

That just really isn't the case. My past is a story. One that comes from a memory in my head that isn't present moment. Presently in this moment, I'm extremely grateful for my parents, who love me, would be willing to read my story, and still love me after hearing the struggles that may have involved them.

My mom especially has been my role model for kindness, compassion, and caring. Someone who meant it when she said, "Your best is enough," and who was there when I needed a cheerleader or a problem solver or just someone to cry with. You are a good mom, Mom. I love you.

A huge deal for me now is to realize I can take all of my experiences and shape the way my kids define "family." My husband (now ex) and I can be an example of love and family, setting a solid foundation for our little dudes to stand on. I might be able to give my kids a model that I didn't have.

It hasn't been easy, and I am still working on it. I catch myself thinking, *You're not doing this right,* or, *This isn't the way normal parents act.* I have to redefine and be with what is going on, daily. I have to learn how to sit on the same page as my husband when it comes to our kids, even though his page looks very different from mine most days.

I struggle constantly to see our common goal. After all, my way is the "right" way. I find myself trying to sell my way to him like I tried to sell running to him, not realizing it's just *my* opinion of what works, not necessarily the *only* opinion.

The key with this stuff is that I'm now aware I'm doing it. That awareness doesn't always prevent me from firing up an argument with my husband, but I do try to think about it now. Marriage and family have been a struggle for me, even with awareness. I desperately want to give my kids a good base to stand on. I also want them to have parents who can teach them about what love is. I feel like I'm only barely figuring that out for myself after forty-three years.

It feels like a huge responsibility.

In 2007, I lost both my grandpa and my dog within ten days of each other. I guess they decided to join forces in heaven. Small pieces of me and my family were lost that week, as shared in the following journal entries.

Journal entry December 12, 2007

Grandpa T.—I remember you looking down at your old-fashioned camera at every family gathering. We have some great pictures because of you. Your house with Grandma in Marin was the greatest. I remember being there with Alissa and always having a fort to play in or tree to climb. I remember your dog, Benji. You helped me build the best dollhouse on a big, flat board with little wood pieces for walls, matchbox dressers, and tiny people. I loved that thing.

When I think of you, I see your smile and how you slapped your thigh when you laughed at something. You were kind and mild-mannered. I see you in your amazing garden in Petaluma and remember how you would hold each flower so gently to show us and have us smell it. I remember walking the train tracks with you and the dog. (Funny how, as I typed the word "dog," it first came out as "God.")

I'm so lucky you were able to meet Danielle and Jonathan. I remember how you held Dani and fed her a bottle like you had done it just yesterday. You seemed strong to me. I knew she was safe in your arms. I know how much you loved us.

Journal entry December 20, 2007
George. You were the best dog! Thank you for watching over us.

Despite the losses, my journal entry at the end of 2007 was uplifting and hopeful.

Journal entry December 30, 2007
This has been a great year, full of fun things and some sad things. Full of things that have challenged me, made me think about life. Started to think about a job change early in the year and realized it wasn't going to happen overnight...I formulated it and shaped it, and here it comes for 2008. That's fine, and it was the original thoughts, I guess. I suppose I will have to work on stronger thoughts.

Jonathan and I have been promoted two belt levels this year and started to get Dani and Dad involved. That has been fantastic. The tournament continues to leave its impression upon me. I can't wait to start up again. I wonder what date I will be writing about the black belt test.

"We can ride the wave of our life whether we are surfing high on top of the wave or whether it is crashing down around us because either way, it is perfection." Laura Di Franco

The year 2008 brought my fortieth birthday and my new private physical therapy practice, a mix of midlife feelings and continued healing. The surf was up in the beginning of this year, as I started to build and get excited about my business. I put much energy into creating the healing space I wanted for my clients and for myself. I had to hold on and ride the waves as the surf came crashing down that year and one of the kids landed in the ER for the first time.

Journal entry January 23, 2008

Three weeks to go before my last day at PT Connection. Mostly excited. Some nervousness. But mostly excited. Three weeks until I turn forty. I feel good about forty.

Watched the black belt test last weekend...Shawn, David, Abe, Diego, Justin, Dean. It was terrifying, and I can't wait.

Journal entry February 14, 2008

Saw my first two patients at Bodyworks. Everything is perfectly right. This's what I'm supposed to do. This's becoming me, clear and perfect.

The weird part is that there doesn't seem to be an attachment to "perfect." There's calm. Grounded. Not charged. Had an appointment with Robin on February 13th, and that was perfect. We talked about it. Talked about Tae Kwon Do and the tournament and the fight of life. The way that becoming more of who you are transcends all parts of your life, not just your work. And I can move along in this life of mine enjoying the wave, whether I'm riding high on top or whether it's crashing down on me, because either way it's perfect.

Journal entry July 10, 2008

On Friday, June 27th, I got a call from Arylawn (where the kids were at summer camp that week). Jonathan had broken his arm in Tae Kwon Do camp. I couldn't believe it. I was racing the ambulance there. Nobody was driving fast enough.

I pulled in behind the ambulance and ran into the building. Jonathan was sitting on the couch in the office cradled in the arms of John, the camp counselor. They both had dazed looks on their faces. Jonathan cried when he saw me, but not too much. The EMT splinted his arm, which was bent abnormally downward in the middle of the forearm, and helped him onto the gurney. I followed the ambulance with Jonathan and John in it to Suburban Hospital.

We all arrived at the hospital, and then the fun began as they tried to start an IV in Jonathan's arm. I think he would have preferred to break his other arm instead of getting an IV. Like mother, like son. First, they missed the vein in his hand—hard to poke a kicking, screaming child, I guess.

After holding him down, they were successful, and he survived. They sedated him so they could set the busted radius and ulna, and he told me mumbled stories about battling the Elite Four in his drug-induced dreams. We finally left the hospital after about three hours, picked up Dani from her sitter Rosa's house, and went home to a hard night's sleep. Daddy was due home the following day from Arizona.

Life is messy. Part of life is realizing you have to deal with death and lots of other crappy stuff. I'd lost a couple of grandparents, my father in-law, an aunt, and an uncle all before this particular year. I didn't feel into those losses like I do now. Aware. The ultimate fear in life is of death.

Speaking of fears, I hadn't tried public speaking as of the writing of this book.

We don't learn about it like math or reading in school. We don't talk about it. We fear it. Mostly because of how we "see" it through our family and teachers and others around us. We whisper about it like if someone hears us, we might be jinxed.

My dear friend Shelly lost her 14-year-old chocolate lab, Spencer, this year, the very same week I lost my aunt Peggy, who was sixty-three. Shelly and I talked about death for a long time. We wondered about it and felt about it and wished we had more answers. She and her family were there on the kitchen floor with their best friend as he passed on. They let go so he could let go.

We can talk about this. We can cry about it. We can bare the heart-sick, throat-clenching feelings about it because we have to and it's life and even death can be okay. Imagine if, as a child, you had a circle of people in your life to be with, to talk to, to feel with, to wonder with, who would talk to you and listen to you about death, and about life. Imagine that kind of family.

Breaking through my thoughts, beliefs, and fears about who I was and who my family was was a huge part of my journey. In the next chapter, I not only break though more limiting beliefs but some boards as well!

Who is your family? How do they celebrate the moments with you?

Use these pages to record your thoughts about the questions at the beginning and end of this chapter...

Go Break a Board

*W*hat have you had to break through in your life?

Being able to break a board with your bare foot or hand is an incredible feeling that's hard to describe. It makes you feel like you can do anything.

I was starting to dabble with breaking through the difficult stuff of my life at this point. I still don't know which hurts more, breaking boards or breaking through the habitual reactions instilled by emotional baggage.

Journal entry December 8, 2007:

I remember when Jonathan and I started Tae Kwon Do almost two years ago and we were watching a group of people test. We didn't know much about testing at that point, and we were mesmerized by it...thinking about how we would be doing that sometime soon.

We stayed after our own class finished to watch everyone complete their test and be promoted. That day, they finished their testing with board breaking. Jonathan was so excited about it that I kept having to "shh" him. He wanted to know if he would be able to do that.

He provided a running commentary on every move the students made. When someone got up to do two boards, he couldn't believe it. What he may not have known right then was that I was about excited as he was.

There's something about this board breaking...about being able to try something you have never done before thinking you might succeed but not being totally sure. Something about being able to break a board makes you stronger, more confident, and something else I can't quite describe. It's totally cool.

Then, on November 20, 2006 (I know this because both my son and I decorated our first broken boards with the date and the words "green stripe"), we did our own test with board breaking at the end. The anticipation of this event was intense. We were about to try to break a real board! For some reason, I wasn't at first sure that the boards were real. When I watched Diego attempt three, I figured they were.

So, even cooler than breaking my board with a jump back kick was watching Jonathan break his with his back kick.

I remember watching a couple of the younger students try and try and try and finally smash them on the floor. I was happy they could leave with a feeling of accomplishment, and I was worried Jonathan wouldn't be able to do it with a back kick.

When he busted through that board, I think my heart exploded. No one ever tells you that your kid's accomplishments and failures are linked directly to your heart. I was so proud of him and still hadn't lost the smile a day later.

We were cool. We got to call all the grandmas and grandpas that night and tell them all about it. We were definitely cool.

Then comes our recent test for the blue belt. Even though you know you can break a board, you think, what if I can't break it today?

The anticipation begins again. Ever since I broke my first board, I've wondered if I could break two. I'm a little competitive. I'd thought about trying it at the Captain's Cup and am so glad I didn't. The anxiety that day was too high. But here was another chance to try.

When it was my turn, Brett was standing next to me waiting to be one of my holders, and I whispered to him that I had always wanted to try two but I wasn't sure. Well, no sooner than I'd let the word "two" out of my mouth, Brett turned around and grabbed a second board. I was really glad he did! I would get to try it!

The first hit was too wide, and I knocked the boards out of Brett's poor hands. Okay, just hit it in the center. The center, I coached myself. "CRACK!" There they went. Totally awesome. That was one of the coolest, most exciting things I have ever done. Even more cool was that my whole family was testing that day, so I had an extra special audience. And an extra special bluish-purple bruise on my right heel for like three days. I better start taking calcium supplements now.

So, hmm next time...maybe three? Hard to imagine it's doable, but it would be worth a try just to see.

I love breaking boards. I figured out during a test one night, after watching one of the students in class break her boards, that I love watching other people break boards too. Especially if they are my classmates.

We know it takes a special combination of aim, concentration, speed, and power to break a board. We have an appreciation for how difficult it is. So we root for others, and we celebrate like it's our victory when they succeed.

I've even caught myself shedding a tear when one of my younger classmates is upset over not being able to break their board. Maybe it's a mom thing, maybe not. I know I'm not the only one who feels it. It goes even further than that.

I read a study that shows that even just watching someone else do something well helps *you* when you do it. So even though we don't practice it all the time, visualizing ourselves succeeding and even watching someone else succeed helps!

I can't wait until the next time I get to break boards, but in the meantime, I will look forward to watching my classmates do it!

Side note: I'm realizing all of a sudden that I've now used words like cool, addicted, awesome, totally awesome, and awesomeness way too many times. You guys get it, though, right? This sport is the best. They need a new word for it. I'm working on that.

I broke three boards with a step side kick on my first try during my last test, which was my third "pretest" for the black belt.

Breaking, as far as I'm concerned, is all about the holders. Your holders need to be big and strong and know what they're doing.

If you have someone who knows how to hold a board and your speed and aim are good, you will break that board. If the person holding your board does not know how to hold it, your chances are decreased.

Another factor in the breaking game is how many people you have holding your boards when you're attempting to break several at once. This can make up for lack of holding experience because of the sheer solidness of the multiple holders versus one holder.

I've been in the middle of breaking boards at a tournament where, after seeing me fail, Master Holloway has come over and either corrected the person holding the board or added his hands to the board. And "Bam!" Done. It's all about the holding.

The other thing I do a lot before I break is visualize the break. I think this helps too, although that is harder to prove.

And then I was faced with a new dilemma: what the heck to do for my black belt test. I wasn't sure I could break three boards. Do I try four? Do I set up something more choreographed? More simple? I love to joke with people about how you know you are addicted to Tae Kwon Do when, as you browse the lumber aisle at Home Depot, you imagine how you'll *break* the wood, not what you'll *build* with it.

The best thing about breaking boards is when you do it, you find out what you're made of. The only time we break boards in Tae Kwon Do is at the end of a test or in a tournament. So unless you practice at home (don't try to practice this at home!), it's mostly unrehearsed. There are such things as re-breakable boards; I own one but have used only it once. It wasn't real enough for me, and my husband refused to hold it after that one attempt when I ended up accidentally hitting his finger.

Because this event is unrehearsed, you have to gather whatever concentration, power, aim, and speed you have in you (which is very little at the end of a test) and focus it into the one quick second of a break, or you will miss. Missing hurts.

I often come away from a sparring match with bruises, but when I have had a bad board-breaking day I'm usually sporting cuts *and* bruises. I have watched some of my friends walk away with broken bones (usually when they attempt the break with their fist or hand).

The part that's thrilling, of course, is when you are successful at something this difficult. If an adult can feel that kind of rush, just think what a kid feels. My eleven-year-old son broke three boards for his black belt test. He succeeded on his third try. He has retold that story many times since. It's worth telling. The confidence that's built through this single part of the sport is amazing.

Every time I go to Home Depot to buy my boards, I think about what I'm about to do. I smell the wood and feel the thickness and heaviness of it, thinking every single time, *Wow, can I do this? What if I can't do this?*

And, of course, I do it every time.

When we break boards in a tournament, the anxiety factor is multiplied. You don't always know who your holders will be, and performing in front of so many people can be frightening.

I learned very, very quickly not to choose a breaking routine that's out of my league or comfort zone for a tournament. Rather, I've learned to tone down my routine due to the extra nerves I usually feel and to be smart about doing a routine that I can accomplish. Because the fact of the matter is that the breaks I've completed over and over in class during tests, I've failed at in tournaments.

Since we've started breaking (Jonathan and I broke our first board for the green stripe on our yellow belt), we've broken one-inch boards. The kids break the same thickness board as the adults, but theirs are a smaller total size. The adults' boards are twelve inches by ten inches, and the kids' are twelve inches by six inches.

In some of the tournaments we've attended, we've seen the kids use what our teacher calls paper boards. I'm not sure what kind of wood they're made out of, but they're very thin.

So, as long as you hit the board, you'll break it. We've been told that a kid competing with thicker boards should score higher. There have been times when we have questioned whether that was happening. Jonathan never asked to use the paper boards, not once, even after coming in second to a kid who broke paper boards over his real ones. Good man.

When you know you can break boards, you know you can do almost anything. Life presents us with many challenges, some akin to what it takes to break a board. Been there, done that, and have used the confidence gained to get past the excuses I was making about not being able to do that next hard thing.

Honestly, I can't think of any real excuse that'll have sticking power at this point. So the only question is, what do I want to do?

In the next chapter, I'll talk about sparring, another part of Tae Kwon Do that truly teaches you what you're made of. Life would forever be labelled as B.S. (Before Sparring) and A.S. (After Sparring).

What if you did something you've never done just to say you did it, especially something you're afraid of?

Use these pages to record your thoughts about the questions at the beginning and end of this chapter...

Life is a Sparring Match

*W*hat have been the "fights" of your life?

The fights, complications, difficulties, problems, and challenges in life end up being incredible opportunities to learn and evolve, but only if you look at them that way. I never learned how to fight, physically or mentally/emotionally as a young person.

I learned how to disappear and not cause problems. There are so many things to worry about nowadays, it feels like a constant fight. Or if you choose to think of it another way, there are so many opportunities to learn, grow, heal, and evolve, it feels like an endless sea of possibilities.

When I was a teenager, my best friend Jenny and I would hang out at Stinson Beach on the weekends and work on our tans. (I can hear my dermatologist gasping as she reads this...) We used baby oil or some form of Banana Boat dark tanning oil to achieve the best possible color and scent of coconut.

We'd lie side by side in our bikinis on our beach towels and talk about boys. We didn't worry about SPF. We didn't even know what that was. In fact, we didn't worry about SPF, wrinkles, cellulite or stretch marks, antioxidants, vitamin B12, tartar, or osteoporosis. We didn't worry about terrorists, suicide bombers, or child molesters. We didn't worry about autism, ADD, irritable bowel syndrome, or impotence. We didn't use the internet, cell phones, DSL, faxes, CDs, iPods, or computers.

Yet somehow we survived high school, college, career, and now family. How did things get so complicated?

The speed of life now seems ridiculous. We are competing against machines. I used to worry about my SAT scores. Now I worry about retirement plans. The drive to always achieve more and be perfect is taking away from the basic need for happiness and loving connections.

I laughed at myself tonight in the bathroom mirror as I got ready to take on my evening routine, including brushing with whitening, tartar control toothpaste; washing my face with a moisturizing cleanser followed by an anti-wrinkle night cream, lip balm, and hand lotion; applying skin-firming cream to thighs, buttocks, and lower abdomen; taking a multi-vitamin and calcium supplement with my third, eight-ounce glass of water; and lying down with a heating pad for my back.

Did I forget to floss?

This routine is accomplished only after making sure the kids have been fed, bathed, brushed, read to, and tucked in. After making their lunches, placing a call to set up their swim lessons, and writing a list of things I need to do this weekend.

Along with this list, there are general behind-the-scenes worries about having enough money to pay for college and retire comfortably, that my relationship lacks intimacy, that the lawn is a bed of weeds, that the furnace needs to be replaced, and that my children may not grow up to be good people because they watch too many cartoons.

Oh, I didn't mention world peace, damn it.

Deep breath.

Journal entry February 10, 2008

I'm wincing from the pain in my shin as I get up on my bed to start writing this note. The bruise there, along with the lump on my elbow and the whiplash feeling in my neck, are all keeping the experience I had in my second Tae Kwon Do tournament from fading too fast. They are definitely making me feel very old. A why-the-hell-are-you-doing-this-to-yourself kind of old.

This time, I felt like I could have used a good therapy session afterward. I ended up spewing out all the details over the phone to my sister that evening. Remember, she's the counselor of my life.

Someone had to hear the details. This time was a reality check for me. No more competing against your classmates who are nice to you.

The first thing I realized is there really aren't many women in my age bracket to compete against, so when you sign up, you take what you can get, no matter the age of the competition sometimes.

The second thing I realized is that I'm not really sure what business I have sparring competitively at this time in my Tae Kwon Do training. I felt unprepared. Mostly for the shots to the head. I do not want to be hit in the head again, ever. At least not without attempting to block it.

That one shot to the head is what prompted my comment about therapy. It wasn't just that I lost. I was proud of the five points I scored. It was the feeling I had that my opponent delivered a shot to the head that was hard enough to knock me down, knowing that she would be warned but also knowing it would throw off my game. And she succeeded, damn it. Psychologically, anyway.

Losing sucked. I would've felt better had I thought I gave it my best fight. My thoughts were mostly on survival during the second round.

Afterward, something happened that I didn't expect. Earlier, Jonathan had walked off the mat of his sparring match in tears after having fought his best fight and losing. No words would console him. My heart ached.

He came around after a while, especially once he realized he would still get a third-place trophy.

After my match, I stood waiting for the others to finish in my bracket, and Jonathan walked up to where I was standing. He asked me if I won and I said, "No, I lost, buddy." He said, "Are you sad?"

With a few tears of my own, I told him, "Remember how you were feeling when you did your match? That's kinda how I'm feeling now."

He looked worriedly into my blurry eyes, and I could tell he knew exactly how I felt. I hoped somehow that would lessen the sadness over his own loss.

Back in November, we'd been able to share some great moments of elation. Today, we shared our moments of defeat. The nice part is that we were able to share at all, connecting a little deeper, and still coming out loving Tae Kwon Do.

In Tae Kwon Do, part of our practice is sparring. We put on full protective gear, face our opponent, bow, and then the fight is on.

In sparring, we are trying to score points by kicking or punching certain scoring areas on our opponent's gear. The chest and the head are the two main scoring areas. In a competition, the person with the most points at the end of the match wins.

So, we're both trying to score points (by kicking or punching), and at the same time we are trying to prevent our opponent from scoring points (by blocking). Sometimes we can also move out of the way fast enough to make our opponent miss (less painful than a block). And so the game goes.

What we really want to avoid is getting kicked in the head (which awards our opponent three points). To not get kicked in the head, you have to practice not getting kicked in the head, which invariably means you will get kicked in the head a few times while trying not to get kicked in the head.

And this is all assuming that your opponent is willing to practice kicking to the head, which some people outright refuse to do (too dangerous). So, to be good at blocking shots to your head, you have to have a sparring partner who is willing to practice kicks to your head. You both have to be willing to take a risk of getting hurt and being the one to inflict the hurt. Crazy, right?

What if, in life, we never had someone who was willing to help us practice like this? The coach, the sparring partner, the husband or wife, the coworker or boss, the friend who would never risk hurting you and so never told you when you could do something better or differently, never gave you feedback on your performance at work, never gave you a more challenging project to do or "stretched" you in any way, never shared their opinion or risked sharing their experience with you, never threw the hard ball, never let you try to see if you could do it?

We practice the art of Tae Kwon Do for fitness, for self-defense, for self-confidence, and to be better people. We count on our classmates and teachers to make us try. They give us the opportunity to stretch our limits, see what we can do, or practice doing things differently.

So why don't we begin to live our lives the same way, helping each other reach a little higher, trusting in our partner's ability, sharing our experiences, teaching what we know, asking new questions, helping each other block a head shot?

The goal is not to hurt your opponent; it's to help them succeed, to do something they never thought they could do, to help them really live in the moment.

All that being said, dear classmates, just because I want to get better at blocking head shots doesn't mean you need to go crazy!

When it comes to sparring, people seem to have a love/hate relationship. There are definitely days when you feel like sparring and days you really don't feel like sparring.

I've found that on the days I really don't want to spar, after I do, I'm glad I did. Kind of like exercise in general when you are feeling unmotivated but motivate yourself to do it anyway, you always feel better afterward.

But with sparring, there seems to be something stronger that can swing your vote in either direction. It's not just fantastic exercise. You have to be present while you spar. You have to think *and* spar. And you can't not pay attention. You can't really fake it, either. It demands your full mind/body effort. And that's why it is so spectacular.

That's also why some days it's difficult to get motivated. I know what it takes, and some days I don't feel I have it in me. I love to spar and I'm afraid to spar, at the same time. I think maybe I love it *because* I'm afraid of it. It makes me feel something, lets me know I'm alive. These types of things become our passions.

When I first received my gear and learned to spar, I felt completely out of control, crazy. Every time I sparred, I was so out of breath that I thought my lungs would explode. I was also not thinking. Ever. It was all full-force craziness.

I feel sorry for those early sparring partners of mine and am grateful for them too. The more I learned, the better it got. I managed to think once in a while, and occasionally my thoughts produced a kick that scored. There was hope.

Now I really look forward to the mind/body practice of sparring, to practicing the things we learn in class to see if we can make them work. And as I relax and play a little, I can do more thinking and kicking at once. It's fun and challenging at the same time.

I want to especially acknowledge all of my black belt sparring partners for your control and patience, but also for knowing when to challenge me. I have improved by sparring people who have been at it a lot longer than I have. Of course, it's more difficult and a little scary to spar someone ranked higher than you, but it's an awesome way to learn new moves and get yourself to step up a notch in your skills.

I've been most appreciative of my sparring practice and partners during the tournaments and exams I've participated in. The partners who have made me work hard, think, and play out of the box have most prepared me for those experiences.

It sounds funny to say that I'm glad when a partner occasionally kicks at my head, but I am. It trains me to block kicks to my head. Believe me, that comes in mighty handy in a tournament when it's not your classmate across from you.

So, if to spar or not to spar is the question...yes would be my answer, even if I don't feel like it. I know I will be better for the practice. If I'm standing in class in the last few minutes of sparring and the teacher says, "Who wants one more round?" I'm always willing to go. One more chance to feel alive, even if I feel like crap as I line up to bow.

When we turn down the opportunity to fight, we have already lost. In the fights of our lives, we can step up and take the chance, and we have at least fifty-fifty odds.

Journal entry August 25, 2008

My baby starts kindergarten tomorrow.
Family dynamics disaster on our vacation.
Family member diagnosed with a terminal illness.
Getting ready for the red belt!
Watching Olympic Tae Kwon Do.

I was glued to the screen watching the Olympics...the color, the bodies, the amazing feats of strength, balance, coordination, speed, and courage. The way the world seems smaller and more friendly. How women looked equal to men. The excitement of competition. The emotion of a win or a loss.

I was moved by the mothers who competed, past their "prime," carving out a new definition of that word. By the coaches who seemed as or more excited by the win than their athlete. I was shocked and saddened by the Tae Kwon Do referee's kick in the face. Sad that there would be any display of poor sportsmanship. I was inspired and motivated to try harder, to ditch my excuses and find out what I am capable of.

I think the fights of our life can be our biggest opportunities. We just have to look at them that way. The trick is to not judge things as good or bad. You never know what the bigger picture might be, even though the current picture seems impossible.

In my healing world, they say we teach what we most need to learn. In the next chapter, my journey progresses to teaching others but also realizing just how much I don't know, and why a beginner's mind is always the place to be in life.

How do you judge the events of your life? And how do you react to them? How is that working for you?

Use these pages to record your thoughts about the questions at the beginning and end of this chapter...

Learning, Testing and Teaching

A*re you still learning? What do you want to learn how to do?*
At this point in time, having earned my red belt, I was using my skills and practice of present moment awareness to be curious, to learn, and to teach. I was enjoying the "tests" of my life—the Tae Kwon Do kind and the other life kind—very much.

Do you ever look up to the sky and ask, "Okay, I give up, is this a test or what?"

At least in Tae Kwon Do, you know when you will be tested. You prepare for it. There's no mistaking it. You show up on time for your test, you do what you are told and perform to the best of your ability. You endure, you sweat, you fall, you get back up again. You know you're being tested, and you've been told what you'll need to do ahead of time. You don't have to second-guess your actions or responses too much.

The tests in life when we aren't completely sure, the what-doesn't-kill-us-makes-us-stronger variety, those are the ones I'm talking about. The God-only-gives-us-as-much-as-we-can-handle kind. Interesting how it was easy to think of two sayings about this kind of thing. We've all had days, months, or even years like that.

Please refer to the chapter on staying in the here and now, as I believe this is the secret to this kind of test, along with a good sense of humor. It goes back to your mind, your thoughts, your emotions, and your reactions to those emotions. It goes back to attitude, and perseverance, and integrity, and indomitable spirit, and, oh wait, those are the tenets of Tae Kwon Do. Go figure.

Many of the opportunities I've had (that felt like a big test at the time) have had to do with saying no and having a voice. The other big tests have been more about speaking from a place inside of me that isn't reacting. In other words, letting the words come from my heart.

One part of this is trusting yourself. Trusting the emotions, the way you feel inside as you make a decision that will affect your future and the future of those you love. Being able to notice and feel those things without reacting is a skill.

Sometimes the tests let you know what you are made of. Our patience can be tested as well as our willpower. I'm mainly interested in the tests where we have to follow our gut to make a decision about our life, to live it from the heart.

When I followed my intuition about not partnering in a bigger business, as I mentioned in the "friends" chapter, I was also forming in my mind the pieces of my career that I *did* want to pursue.

I knew I wanted to teach, both workshops for teaching people how to heal their bodies and eventually Tae Kwon Do. I felt so passionate about this and knew it was what would fill me up.

What I didn't know in that moment of following my heart and sending that email to my friend was how the universe would align to answer my request a bit later in a different way. Now, a year and a half later, I'm teaching classes and workshops in all the areas I desired. I'm able to keep a fantastic life/work/family balance, and I love it. I still dream of a martial art healing center and know if it's meant to show up, it will. I'm learning to trust it all.

It's *all* a test, people! A test to see if you're awake. To see if you're awake to the stuff of your life. If you can live that life from your truth. Your true self. One moment at a time. And not get sucked into the black hole of your mind chatter that says you aren't good enough, or you aren't this or that enough.

I start to get louder inside when I write this stuff, like I think you aren't listening. I start to get excited and type faster and get louder because I want anyone who needs it to know they can make choices for their life, if they are awake for it. Deep breath. Here is a note about Tae Kwon Do.

Journal entry September 27, 2008

Adrenaline rush, can't get enough
Did 100 kicks
Did 100 leg lifts
I've been kicked in the head and punched in the face
Can't get enough
Tested seven times, busted seven boards
Entered in two competitions
Did too many push ups

Tougher than I was, but still terrified
Olympian at heart

Testing my limits
Always pushing harder
Every day is an opportunity
Kicking higher, stronger
Wishing I were taller
One with the moment
New form to master
Doing my best
Only one belt to go.

An actual Tae Kwon Do test is quite an event. The ultimate goal of the test is a promotion to the next belt color/level. Most of my friends (myself included) have a fair amount of nerves before a test.

You learn most of the different components of the test in class, but the nerves are about being able to remember everything. And a little about being able to break your boards. Board breaking is the only thing we do not practice before a test.

We are tested by being asked to perform basic kicks, a series of punches, kick combinations, our fundamental moves for the form we've learned and the form itself.

We spar, and we break boards. Sometimes we practice sparring maneuvers or self-defense techniques. The forms are performed as a group, and our highest form is done individually.

We're also required to turn in an essay on the day of the test. The essay can be about anything you want. You can't test unless you turn it in. The list I have made includes the usual routine. The tests where this varies are always interesting. Just when you think you know what's coming up, you're asked to do something else.

As a color belt, white up to red, we do a "regular" test with our classmates at the YMCA, where we take our weekly classes, that usually takes about an hour or an hour and a half (the same length as a regular class).

When we're ready, Master Holloway invites us to join the "black belt test," which takes place twice a year at his dojang.

The black belt test includes all of the Gentle East black belts of varying degrees, and any red belts that have been invited to test there. I've been part of four of these tests to date, the longest so far lasting five hours.

When you participate in a test that lasts five hours, the test becomes an endurance event and is much more intense, both physically and mentally.

Nutrient timing becomes a skill, with muscles doing crazy things they never usually do. Thoughts must be focused, or they overwhelm. These tests are hard. That's the point. If they weren't hard, we wouldn't have the satisfaction of knowing that we really earned that belt.

I love them. I think they show us who we really are and what we're capable of. They've forced me to learn more about my body, about how to fuel it properly and prevent dehydration, and how to focus my mind and prevent giving up. Like that's an option.

At the end of a five-hour test when every part of you is spent, you are then asked to break boards. You've spent some time beforehand thinking about the breaking routine you would like to perform, how many boards you'll break, where they will be placed, etc...

What I never usually think about until I'm there is the fact that my legs have nothing left by then. It takes an unusual amount of determination and resolve to put what you have left of balance, speed, power, and aim into your kicks at that point and have it be enough to break the boards.

Sometimes it doesn't happen. Sometimes you have to change your plan when the original one doesn't work. Sometimes you break something other than the board. Knocking on wood, this has not happened to me.

When I began reading about martial arts, searching websites, going to tournaments, and talking to people, I realized that not all Tae Kwon Do schools and teachers are the same.

I learned about black belt factories. You know those places where you see tiny black belts running around? *What's the point of this,* I wonder? How can wearing a black belt mean anything if you don't truly earn it by some blood, sweat, and tears?

I'm really thankful that when I talk about the belt I've earned in a recent test, I can honestly say I worked for it and know it meant something.

Journal entry December 21, 2008

Our red belt test went very well yesterday. All of our classmates did great! Jonathan and I had it all down. Well, we had had it all down for a while. I should have just done two boards. My back kick board break looked awesome. Dad got a great picture of it and of Jonathan too. It feels good to be a red belt!

Journal entry January 11, 2009

It was great to be back in TKD class yesterday after the holiday break. Master Hathway taught all three classes solo but asked me to start the 10:30 a.m. class. It was a great way to break in my red belt! I love TKD. I'm sore today.

Over the years, I have used a simple writing exercise when I am not sure what else to write about or focus on. It is the acronym IAGF, which stands for I Am Grateful For...

Here is my IAGF from January 18, 2009

Connecting on a truer level
Red, and purple
Shelly
Helicopter kicks
Being with my kids who want to be with me

Red Belt Essay November 2008

I'm sitting here looking at a very large purple bruise on my elbow that I managed to make by trying to break a board yesterday at the tournament, and I'm wondering how much longer my body will let me do this. I hope forever.

Maybe if I start taking calcium now, I can ensure a long board-breaking career. Since there were only two other female board breakers in my age category, I realize this will be a lonely career. Fun and lonely. I can't let a lack of other motivated (crazy) middle-aged women slow me down. So I decided that I won't. Slow down, that is.

I decided after yesterday that I only want to speed up. Use my body to its full ability for as long as humanly possible, that's the goal. Why not? What do I have to lose? Well, a broken arm or leg and lost wages I guess, but bones heal. If you don't try, you only end up with regrets. Regrets are harder to deal with psychologically. Bones are easy to deal with if you have a good orthopedist.

Since I know a few good orthopedists, I decided I can't slow down. It's too darn fun to speed up, to give things your best shot and have fun with the results. And learn and grow and get better.

I enjoyed sparring and losing yesterday (after dealing with severe anxiety for at least an hour once I realized that I had agreed to spar against a black stripe gal in the tournament).

It would have been awesome to win the match, but I enjoyed the match itself and conquering my fear of sparring, my fear of getting nailed in the head, and my fear of failing. In the end, I lost, but I also gained a lot.

It was my husband who talked me into agreeing to the match. This was a big deal. I was amused by his excitement over it and his support of me. He then went and rallied the troops, and over walked Brett and Diego to form my cheering section. How could I say no at that point?

The adrenaline rush during the waiting for the match to begin was the worst thing of all. My heart pounded so hard for so long that I think it took everything out of my legs. And even though I was faster and more agile than my opponent, I couldn't score enough points to win. I had fun, though. A lot of fun this time. I would do it again just to remind myself that I can do just about anything that I'm afraid of. If I had gone home without sparring, I would have regretted it.

So thank you, Master Holloway, for giving us all the opportunity to compete, to give our best fight, to learn and grow. It was fantastic to be a part of your tournament; to be among the amazing Masters, coaches and referees there; to be a part of the camaraderie of our Gentle East team; and to get a chance to practice what you have taught us.

I was learning a new definition of excellence, and the following poem came from that new perspective.

Nothing is Something

My story of excellence is a story. Nonfactual. Not true.
My definition of excellence is only a point of view.
Also not true.

It might be right, but it is still not true.
Can I let go, even when I am right?
Can I let go of my right to be right?
Yes, I can let go.
Even when it is hard.
My choice is to let go
especially when it is hard,
especially when I am right.
Those moments become the gift
to myself and to the other
because they make something into nothing.
And nothing is the ultimate possibility of something.
It is just that I don't know
what that something is yet.
I let go of the need to know
because I know if I let go
I will have the gift of something.
Something good.

Once you receive a black stripe on your red belt, you're then in preparation mode for the black belt test. At Gentle East, we must then complete at least three more tests called pretests, which earn us three more black stripes on one side of the belt. Master Holloway then lets us know if we are eligible to take our black belt exam.

The examination for my first black stripe was the first time I'd joined the group of black belt and fellow red belt students at Gentle East to test, rather than testing at YMCA, which is our usual place of practice. I'd gone to watch one of these tests as a green belt out of curiosity. Part of me left wishing I hadn't gone, I was so terrified. Part of me left glad I had gone, to feel prepared.

I've now been a part of four of these tests and struggled with wondering how much to tell other red belts when they ask me about it, not wanting to taint their experience but also knowing that just because it was a certain way for me does not mean it will be that way for them (learned that one the hard way a couple times). So I currently answer questions as directly as possible without adding details.

One of the amazing things you learn as you advance in rank and observe the students who are ranked higher than you is that there's always something to learn.

I love to teach, so when I take a class, I'm not only learning and practicing for myself but I'm also paying attention to how certain things are taught. A five-year-old white belt learns one way; his 38-year-old dad learns another.

I enjoy listening to my instructors as they teach, watching the tricks they use to make people understand, witnessing the way they go about allowing students to figure things out, and learning the variety of ways they do this.

To earn some spending money while I was going to physical therapy school, I taught aerobics at two or three local gyms. One of my favorite things to do to learn new moves was to go take a class somewhere else from a different instructor. I liked changing the routine often enough to keep myself and my students excited about it.

Now, with my physical therapy practice, I take continuing education every year and I also work with other colleagues to learn new techniques. Sometimes we trade services. Sometimes we get together in study groups. The fact that there'll always be something else to learn is what makes what I do exciting. If you really want to learn something, teach it.

I watched Master Holloway in class the other day going back and forth between the row of black belts and our row of red belts, then to the row that had a green belt and a yellow belt. We were working on kick combinations and then forms.

Every belt up to red has two different kick combinations, and no two are alike. Each combination has at least five different kicks in it. The red belts with black stripes have four kick combinations, and some of us have two additional kick combinations that we have created.

From white to red, there are nine different forms, each with a different and random number of moves. The black belts have an additional number of forms beyond those nine, depending on their degree rank. Master H. knows it all without looking at a notebook. He works the room and keeps everyone going.

One day I hope I'll be able to pull the combinations out of my brain at will. There's a lot more to learn.

Journal entry June 14, 2009

Black stripe test for Saturday...have been doing a lot of practicing. Jonathan is ready and testing with Stephanos, which is good. I'm ready and am testing at Gentle East, which makes me nervous and excited. I need to arrange my board-breaking routine. Jump side kick with two boards and jump back kick with two boards. Or jump side with two, reverse turning with one, 360-degree back kick with one. That's it, maybe.

Black Stripe Essay June 20, 2009

When Ms. M first asked me to help her by warming up the class, I was surprised but excited. I love helping. I love teaching. I'm lucky I get to teach every day in my day job. I love to help people learn something they didn't know before then. I especially love to help people learn something physical that they have never done before.

Being able to give people a perspective they haven't thought of that helps them to have a new understanding of how to maneuver their body to make something happen is fun. Their successes become yours. I appreciate that each person I meet learns differently and have tried to think of different ways to say something or show something so that I can help more people. Being able to teach everyone equally well is difficult. Sometimes I try to remember that not everyone will get it or be in tune with my teaching style.

In my job, I'm usually able to help almost everyone learn, but occasionally it doesn't click. Over time, I've asked myself to relax on those days so I don't end up being hypercritical or excessively pessimistic on myself.

It would be nice to help everyone, but I sometimes wonder if that's a realistic goal. When you become a Master, can you literally help anyone learn a move?

I can enjoy warming up the class because I know the moves and can describe them with some accuracy so that everyone knows what to do. After you do something enough times, you have it memorized to a point that you don't have to think about it when you teach it. Then you can be creative. You can flow. You can answer questions, change the movement slightly, customize it for the person, and then come back to the beginning again.

I've enjoyed knowing enough Tae Kwon Do to be able to help others learn it. I would love to be able to flow with the teaching. I'm honored when people ask me a question. I only hope I can teach it right.

I've also especially enjoyed learning from the different instructors and other students in our classes. There was a time when a thought of dread might have gone through my head when I knew I was coming up against certain people in class to spar with. I'd be worried about them being too big, too tall, too advanced, not advanced enough, etc. Now I try really hard to go at it with the attitude of "what can this person help me learn?" And the beauty of it is that with each person it's different, which means I get to learn something new with every person I'm with.

It's helpful to learn the energy of different people and the way we can get caught up in someone else's energy. If someone is tired and slow, you can get dragged into it. If someone is sharp, intense, and hyper, you can get caught up in that, too.

Working with the person by moving and engaging can work to your advantage or disadvantage. Either way, I learn how to move with that person and their style. For the same reason, it is also great to have three different instructors teaching the different classes. Each person's teaching style is slightly different and helps you in different ways. It's the same in life.

You need to understand how to communicate with all types of people, teachers, parents, students, colleagues, etc. Being able to flow with all kinds of personalities is helpful, interesting, and sometimes frustrating. When I use that attitude of "what can I learn from this person today," though, the frustrating ones become more interesting.

Everything I learn can be used to help someone else learn. In my mind, I used to be in a race for the end goal all the time. Now I'm happily enjoying the journey and the nuggets I get to find along the way. Things are more interesting and way less stressful that way. Ultimately, if I can teach people that very thing, I will be glad.

Journal entry June 22, 2009

I was very happy to be a part of the Gentle East test on Saturday. I'm glad we delayed our trip. For me, it was worth it to be a part of this group, which ended up being smaller than usual, they said. Only twelve people.

I met Lois, David, Shawn, Master Lee, brothers Victor and Steven, Adam, Peter, Alejandros, Justin, and Susan's son—I can't remember his name. It was really good to have the test out of the way. The next one will be different with the first out of the way. I have to read about fueling my legs. I did feel like I had a bit of a second wind somewhere in there. It felt psychological, though. Like now or never. I can't wait until the next one. I have to practice my forms.

In the next chapter, I dabble with another kind of teacher: gratitude.

Are you teaching what you know? If not, why not?

Use these pages to record your thoughts about the questions at the beginning and end of this chapter...

Grateful

Do you live in gratitude?

There's power in gratitude. I learn this more and more every day as I practice it. I started to feel how using gratitude as a daily focus kept my life positive and hopeful, even when it was difficult or depressing. If you want your life to change, start mastering the art of feeling grateful no matter what's happening in your life.

> *"You cannot exercise much power without gratitude because it is gratitude that keeps you connected with power." Wallace Wattles*

In one of our sessions, a patient shared something a friend said to her about being present to your thoughts:

"When you realize all the crap that is going on in your head, just flush the toilet."

Man, I loved that. It's so true. The other thing you can do is replace the crap with the feeling of being grateful for what you have.

I've mentioned being grateful in a few sections of this book before this, as it's been a really important part of the shift I made in my thinking. And it changed the way I thought and felt about my life. I continue to be grateful for everything as often as possible.

I've thought about showing my appreciation for the things and people in my life in different ways. With a focus like this, everything seems right and life seems more enjoyable, especially in the moments it could otherwise seem boring, difficult, frustrating or downright fucked up. I remember learning the art of the thank you note from my mom. Thanks, Mom; that was really important.

The year 2009 was when I decided to get all the Tae Kwon Do students together to say thanks to our instructors with a party. I wanted them to know how much we all appreciate what they do for us. The dedication, patience, and commitment they have to this sport and to us is incredible. I really felt moved to acknowledge it.

So I rallied the troops, and together we planned a Tae Kwon Do celebration for Master Holloway, Master McDermott, and Master Hathway.

I wrote up an invitation to all the classes, handed it out secretly after classes, organized a potluck lunch, and made up a little TKD presentation for the teachers.

Diego started us off by letting the instructors know why we had gathered. The kids each held a card with one of the letters of the word Tae Kwon Do on it and read the sayings that we had made up. We had a little Tae Kwon Do trivia, and then we feasted on a wonderful potluck lunch that all the parents had contributed to. It made me really happy to say thank you like that.

The following were the cards that the kids held up, each de-scribing something the instructors do for us each time they teach.

T Terrific things you teach us
A Amazing ability to bring out the best in your students
E Experience and excellence in your art
K Killer kicks we've learned
W Wisdom, willingness, and way you help
O Outstanding amount of patience you have
N Never letting us quit
D Driving us toward the dream of the black belt
O Overall, over-the-top, high-octane class you give us each and every week!

Journal entry November 19, 2009

We pulled off the Tae Kwon Do party, and it was a super awesome success. The instructors were happy, and a whole slew of students showed up to help me. I'm glad I put the effort into this. It was overdue.

Where are thanks overdue in your life?

"Look for something to appreciate." Esther Hicks

Living from a grateful place every day is so important. I learned if you want something for yourself and you see that another person has it, feels it, achieved it, is celebrating it, has been there and done that, the best thing to do is get completely caught up in the positive energy of it with them.

Help them achieve it, help them celebrate. You will attract that kind of energy to yourself in so doing. Don't be jealous, get mad, be angry, feel sorry for yourself, wonder why it's always them and never you, or isolate yourself. Be grateful for what you have. That's the law of attraction: like attracts like. If you're grateful, you'll attract more to be grateful about.

I recently felt an example of this during Tae Kwon Do class. A friend of mine in class is a great writer. She has a wonderful blog and has written for various magazines. Master Holloway announced in class the other day that she was going to have an article published in a local magazine about the first sport she ever participated in, Tae Kwon Do!

Damn, why didn't I think of that? I thought. I'm only human, after all. Very quickly, I realized that the "look what she did, I'm no good" attitude was going to get me absolutely nowhere.

I wrote her an email that night (I know she is laughing as she reads this) and congratulated her, letting her know how excited I would be to read her article. And I am! If I can harness the fabulous energy that she must be feeling and celebrate those emotions and feelings with her, I will be creating it inside of myself, rather than creating frustration and disappointment.

Get it?

In case you don't totally get it, here's the science: when you feel an emotion, your body releases chemicals that are that emotion's signature. When you're angry, you release that anger into yourself in the form of chemicals, which are energy. So, in effect, what you're doing is negatively affecting your own body, mind, and soul when you're practicing negative emotions that create stress in the body.

The idea would be to choose the emotions, like gratitude, that have a healthy, positive effect on your body, mind, and soul.

We have to practice supporting each other. We have to give more. Each without the expectation of getting anything in return. We can feel the positivity, love, joy, celebration, and success inside, like it's our own. And it will be. It is already. And science is helping us realize that this is a way more healthy way to go about things.

So I try to say "thank you" as often as possible. Because my body can't tell the difference between whether it's me or the other person when I'm experiencing gratitude. Either way, the energy of gratitude is released into me.

In fact, if I find myself feeling blue or particularly judgmental, I usually sit and think about who in my life I can write a thank you note to. There's always someone, and doing this shifts your mind to a state of being grateful.

We can say thank you in big ways, like our party, and in really small ways, like a note or a phone call. Do what you can with what you have from where you are to say, "Thanks." Sometimes when I'm at the store, I will spend a couple minutes in the card aisle and stock up on my thank you notes, just for the heck of it, whether I have someone in mind or not.

Here is another one of my "I Am Grateful For" journal entries:

IAGF
Dog sniffs and wags
Warm weather, windows open
Bird songs in the morning
Giggling kids cracking themselves up
Recognizing thoughts as nothing
Intuition
Helping people decrease pain

The thing about being grateful is that no matter who you are or what circumstance you are in, there is always something to be grateful for. The list might just look very different. This perspective will instantly change you to feeling grateful; you just have to remember to think it.

IAGF
A house with heat in the winter
Clean water to drink
Clothes to wear
Food to eat
Someone to talk to
Someone to love

Maybe the list needs to be shorter:
I am grateful for being alive.
Kind of puts everything else into perspective.

Ever since I learned about the law of attraction, I've practiced being and feeling grateful. At first, it's something you have to remind yourself to do. Later, it just becomes the way you feel most of the time. Eventually, this attitude shines out from you and is the way you live. When people talk about changing the world one person at a time, this is part of it. So use any opportunity you have to say thank you. Start a gratitude journal. Switch to gratitude any time you are feeling sorry for yourself. Help others without any expectation of reward. Imagine how you can inspire others, and then do it!

"If the only prayer you ever say in your entire life is thank you, it will be enough." Meister Eckhart

This idea is so simple. Now, if you're ready, let's level up from gratitude to pure passion. In the next chapter, I'm playing with my passions and working on being unapologetic about living in them, in gratitude.

What are you grateful for today?

Use these pages to record your thoughts about the questions at the beginning and end of this chapter...

Passions

hat totally lights you up?

Finding and feeling passion for something is a discovery like no other. Passion grounds you in the present moment and does it while lighting a fire inside you that fuels your continued pursuit of that passion. I've had several passions in my life. It was eventually the ones I decided to make my life about that mattered the most.

"One person with passion is better than forty people merely interested."
E.M. Forster

When I was growing up, my dad had a 1965 Mustang. It was a hard top, light blue. I loved that car and wanted one for myself really badly, even before I was old enough to drive. I'm not really sure what it was about it, but cars in general are exciting to me.

By the time I could drive, my parents were divorced and my dad's Mustang was long gone. I begged for one of my own and had been working at the local pizza place since I was fifteen to save my money to help pay for it.

My mom and I found a bright red 1966 hard top for sale that year, and my best friend's dad, a used car salesman, came to check it out with us. We paid $1,000, and I had my first car.

Well, turns out that you need a lot of time and money to keep a classic car in working order, and since we had little of both, we eventually had to sell the car after it sprung an oil leak one day. I went through at least three other used cars I can remember: the Datsun pick-up truck that had a cracked engine block, the Honeybee, and a dark blue Honda Prelude. The last one lasted through my years at college. They all paled in comparison to that Mustang, though, as far as I was concerned.

In college, I dated a guy who worked for the local radio station and often got tickets to local sporting and cultural events. He came around one day with tickets to The Winston Cup NASCAR race at Sears Point in Napa, California, near where I grew up. We watched the race from a special booth set up at one of the "crash" corners. I remember not being able to look away as the cars roared and squealed by.

There were all kinds of spin outs at our turn, and it was thrilling to watch the drivers recover and keep going. One of the most exciting parts was watching the cars screech into pit row and then watching the crews going at their work as fast as humanly possible. I wished I could drive one of those cars!

I wished that wish for twenty-seven years. I have, in my older age, driven various cars, including a Saturn, Jeep, Miata, Passat, Explorer, and Lexus. But never a NASCAR.

One Christmas morning, after the kids opened their presents and my husband and I had been through our own, I could hear him whispering to Danielle. She brought me one last gift, a white envelope with a purple Matchbox car taped to the top. Dani was excited as she explained that the car changed colors if you got it wet, or something like that. I was too excited to listen to her...I knew what was in the envelope.

On May 15, 2010, I'd be going to the raceway in Richmond, Virginia, and after attending an orientation and class, I would be getting into my fire suit and helmet and taking eight laps in a NASCAR, which I was told could reach speeds of up to 160 miles an hour.

Best. Present. Ever!

Some ladies get jewelry. Too bad for them.

We arrived at the track early and drove through a short tunnel onto Pit Road. I could already hear the roar of the cars, and I had goose bumps. I checked in and was told to get suited up in the classroom. I was given a fire suit and helmet, and then it was time to join the other students (which consisted of nine men) in the classroom.

Mr. Ed Lane was there to teach us all about the track, following the line, a technique called "left and lift," the flags and passing. I'm pretty sure I heard most of it, but I was so nervous that I really struggled to stay in the moment.

"At the first cone, you lift off the accelerator, second cone break gently, third cone slowly build up speed again."

Do this at turn two and turn four. Or was it one and three? "Stay as high up and as close to the wall as possible on the straightaway and down as low as you can in the turns."

Oh my God, I won't be able to remember anything, I remember thinking. I think he said to remember to relax and have fun, too.

We headed into the van for a tour of the track and to review the line. *Cone one...what are we supposed to do again?* I thought. *Oh yeah, off the accelerator. Am I going to be able to do this?*

Then back into the pit and time to wait our turn to drive. It was 1:00 p.m., and the noon group was just starting! The wait was a killer. I watched the other amateur drivers getting into cars and the professional drivers taking willing participants on their "Ride Along" experiences. I wondered if it was ever going to be my turn.

"Laura?" I heard my name finally, and it was time to head to car number seven. This was it. The guy who was there to help guided me across Pit Road to the car. "Are you nervous?" he asked.

Ha! I confessed that I was totally nervous, but I also noticed something interesting. I was not the usual shaky, heart pounding, crazy nervous. I was just completely excited. Comfortably excited. I was ready. This was going to be totally awesome.

I climbed into the car through the window and down into the seat and realized I was staring at the dashboard. So after four extra pads were put under and behind me, I could finally see over the front of the car and reach the pedals!

The harness was really tight, with five heavy metal clips across the front and lap. I was literally glued to the seat back.

"Go ahead and start the car," the helper said. That was accomplished by flipping a switch located on the left part of the dash. I reached my left hand out, and my fingers stopped short. Even with all the extra pads, I was still too short to reach the ignition switch!

So my helper turned on the car while I gave it some gas and "vrooooommmmmm!" went that NASCAR! The vibration enveloped my body from the seat under my butt and from the steering wheel through my hands and arms, and I got more goosebumps, the full-body kind!

I tucked two headphone ear pieces in between my helmet and ears and could hear the track director shouting orders. "Go seven. Go! Go seven!" My heart was beating so hard, I could feel it through the fire suit.

I shifted into gear and followed the van for the first lap, again to review the line and to practice "left and lift," which is a passing drill. I could feel my entire body tightening in excitement and remembered he said to relax! Then the van disappeared and the green flag appeared.

I never looked at the speedometer or the rearview mirror. I have no idea how fast I was going or who was behind me. All I knew was that nobody was in front of me. It took me five or six laps to finally realize that the back end of the car was not going to float off the track and that I didn't really have to use the brake at all if I did it right.

All I could think was that I was driving a race car! During the second to last lap, the two professional drivers on the track doing ride alongs passed me on the outside, so fast that I felt like I was standing still. Time to chase!

I did everything I could to keep their back bumpers in my sight for the last two laps. It was awesome and scary. And then I saw the checkered flag. Time to come into the pit. Bummer!

I rolled in and stopped with the biggest ever shit-eating grin on my face. I could feel sweat dripping down my face and my back.

"How was it?" my helper asked.

"Totally, totally awesome!" I replied.

I didn't want to get out. For those eight laps, nothing else existed except me, the car, and the track. Like being sucked into the moment by adrenaline and sheer joy at the same time.

I swear it was like God picked me up, plopped me down right in the middle of bliss, and then yanked me back out again. I know that driving a race car isn't everyone's idea of bliss, but it was a dream come true for me. I was so in the moment, I did not feel like I was in my body. Wait, can that happen at the same time? Can you be in the moment and out of your body all at once? That's exactly how I felt.

I so want to do it again. I want to feel like that again. For now, I accept this other feeling; I go back to my normal life as a 42 year-old wife, mother, and physical therapist, and I feel, as unattached as possible, I feel. And it's good, too.

The thing that lights you up...that's passion. Those are the things to pursue in your life, because those are the things that bring out the true joy in you. When the true joy is being expressed, it's the closest to being your truest essence as a human. in the chapter for myself

Passions can be big or small. I've found it pleasurable to have more than one, but one is enough. Passion goes beyond love. I love chocolate. But I don't want to be with it, write about it, make it, buy it, and think about it in every moment. I also love my family. Oh, this is a tricky one. Yes, they light me up. It isn't the same. The things that I'm passionate about allow me to feel joy independent of everything and everyone else. They are pure joy. We ache for them. I think if your passion is a person, it would be called obsessive. Hmm. Passion. Obsession. Where do we draw the line?

I am passionate about Tae Kwon Do, and I've been obsessed, yes, at times when it has come to needing rest (and my resistance to taking that rest). Mostly, it's become a way of living. I'm passionate about horses too. Being near them is a healing thing for me, but I don't obsess.

The definitions of the two words from Webster:

> "Obsession—a persistent disturbing preoccupation with an often unreasonable idea or feeling."
> "Passion—an intense driving or overmastering feeling or conviction."

Disturbing and unreasonable are the words that help you know the difference.

So, can I be passionate about my children? Can my children be one of my passions? I'm passionate about them, but they are not a passion in the same way horses or Tae Kwon Do or cars are. As I write this, I'm still not sure.

And because you're reading a new edition of this book right now, here's what I want to add about passion, and the feeling of it inside you. It's up to you to feel things like joy and passion, no matter what you're doing in your life. Even though we can and should pursue the things, people, and situations that bring us joy, it doesn't mean we can't feel joy just because.

We have control over our feeling at all times. I used to think I'd have to do certain things (like drive a race car) to feel joy. Today, I know that all I have to do to feel joy is stand here and feel joy. My joy factor has been up-leveled. It's liberating to know it's up to me. I'm in control of how I feel.

Here is a poem I wrote shortly after I cantered on a horse for the very first time. I let this little piece of me shine out in words the best I could. I wanted to share the feeling I had with people.

Learning How To Fly

Guinness taught me how to fly,
From walk to trot to take-off
He knew his job
No matter where my feet were in the stirrups
Or how much I fumbled with the reins,

He lifted me into the sky.
And then I felt the rhythm
And sank into my heels and spread my wings
And we were two spirits alive with each other
One heart together.
I was breathless
Not from exhaustion but exhilaration, pure joy.
I WAS joy
With my mustang boy
Who nibbled at me in waiting
To tell me that he was a good soul.
I hope I live many more days
To fly this way
In powerful rhythmic breath, only present to the moment
Which is pure delight.
Only knowing that, over and over and over again.

When I feel passion or joy, I write about it and talk about it and share it and think about it. I want to find someone else who is passionate about it so that I can talk about it some more. Okay, sounding obsessive. Here is where I get into trouble in the big spiritual picture of things. I get attached to elation. I want the passion feeling—and who wouldn't—but I want it all the time, like it's the "better" way to be.

I struggle with the downers; they're a bad way to feel, need to change it, get me out of it quick. This gets back to my comment about being able to see the big picture in the middle of chaos. It's about not judging your circumstance and also not identifying with it. Yeah, easy for Robin, or Eckhart, or Ingrid, or Dr. Wayne to say. Not easy to do.

In Oriah Mountain Dreamer's book *The Invitation*, she says, "Avoid being self absorbed. The most profound self knowledge is gained by staying awake to our thoughts and feelings and actions during the fires of daily living. Remember that you are not the pain, not the anxiety. Let something larger than yourself take you as you are, every day, every moment, hand it over." And remember the bigger picture.

Journal entry January 22, 2010:

First pretest. There were fourteen of us, including three men from Florida. Dean, Diego, and Peter earned their black belts tonight!

I remember being part of this test, my first pretest for the black belt, thinking how lucky I was to be part of this group of cool people and how proud I was of my three classmates from the Y who were earning their black belts that night.

By this time, the passion that I felt about Tae Kwon Do was big, and realizing that some of the classmates I'd trained alongside of were reaching this ultimate goal motivated me and fueled my fire about it in a big way. I was going to have a chance to watch *and* be a part of their achievement, while wondering what it would feel like for myself.

By the end of that night, I was the only red belt and one of only two women standing among my peers. I love that particular photograph. I was very proud to be standing there with so much experience and dedication surrounding me. So much passion. I might have been floating a little.

The people I train with are not just classmates, they're my friends. We share this crazy passion for Tae Kwon Do. When you have been practicing, training, and testing together—not to mention sweating on each other—for five or six years, you start to get to know each other a little bit.

You know some things about their personalities and a lot about the way they spar, if you've been paying attention. When you show up for class and one of your friends isn't there, you miss them. Class isn't the same without your comrades.

In Tae Kwon Do, this kind of friendship bond forms I think because each person has an appreciation for the dedication and physical and mental strength it takes to persevere in this sport. These people have seen your worst day along with your best, and they cheer for you on both.

In daily practice, you're competing against yourself, trying to do a little better each time. Your classmates help you do that. They are your sparring partners, they hold the boards that you break, they sweat and kihap (yell) and grunt alongside of you.

A "Good job!" or "Congratulations!" after a test from them makes you smile. You know they know. It means what it means because of them.

I'm happy now to be able to say that I feel passionate about several areas of my life, including my job.

I began my career back in 1994 and developed an intense passion for healing. My journey has been all about it. It's really why I chose to write in the first place; I wanted to collect all my stories, in case they would make someone smile or help them see something in a different way. And my own healing has been about rediscovering and expressing my voice.

The influences in my life go back to my high school career center, in particular the day I signed up to listen to the physical therapist speak about the profession. As I mentioned earlier, I connected way back then with her energy and enthusiasm about it. She was excited and happy being able to help people.

I've learned so much about life through this path. Becoming a physical therapist allowed me to earn my license to touch. Connecting with my strength—that I've always been passionate about inspiring people to be healthy and love their life—gave me purpose.

Health is so much more than not feeling sick or being in pain. It's feeling awake inside your life, being able to feel everything, and bringing your truth out into the world to connect with others, for love and for joy.

And maybe it includes a little bit of passion.

I listened to a talk by Brené Brown in which she said connection is why we're on the planet. We must connect to feel alive. I spent so much of my earlier life doing things to achieve, to get ahead, to make more money, to do what I thought I was supposed to do. Now connection is what I'm drawn to.

When I connect with others, whether it's through work during a physical therapy session or at Starbucks when the tone of my voice and the smile in my eyes helps my "thank you" mean something, I feel good.

Sometimes connecting helps the other person, and sometimes it helps me. Sometimes I meet someone because I chose to connect and an opportunity presents itself that seems unbelievable.

This example might seem too easy, but it was one of the moments I felt like connection was why I was alive. One of the women I know because of Tae Kwon Do is a fifth-degree black belt. She sought me out one day because of a problem she was having in her knee. In our discussions, she was telling me about an impending move for her job and that she was going to have to give up teaching a Tae Kwon Do class that she started for a local recreation center.

I'm sure I was beating around the bush with how I was responding but finally came around to letting her know I was very interested in teaching. By the end of her physical therapy session, we were both excited about the possibility of me being able to take over her class. I had doubts (and still do) about my skills and confidence level, but realizing that this amazing, kind, and experienced teacher thought I would be a good fit for the job was really, really cool.

Continuing to Learn

To keep my license as a physical therapist in the state of Maryland, I'm required to take a certain amount of continuing education. My earliest mentors and my choices for continuing education make me the physical therapist I am today: somewhat alternative, definitely holistic.

My focus through the last five to ten years has been craniosacral therapy and myofascial release, both mentioned earlier. My passion and interest for more holistic, mind-body forms of evaluation and treatment was stimulated when Michele Hunter, my first mentor, taught me how to do a sphenoid (one of the bones in your skull) release, and it made our patient's headache disappear.

I wanted to be able to do more of that! I took as many classes as I could afford every year to become that kind of therapist. The following journal entry describes a cold morning in February, three days after my birthday, in Sedona, Arizona, where I took *Myofascial Unwinding*, one of *those* kinds of continuing education courses.

Journal entry February 18, 2010:

With a coffee in hand, I walked down past my room down the road that continued into the nearby neighborhood. It was just before sunrise and chilly. I wore my coat, gloves, hat. I found the creek that the cab driver told me about behind a handful of beautiful Sedona homes. I hoped nobody would wake up and find me traipsing through their yard in my black hat as I made my way to the creek.

So I found a place on a huge tree trunk that was lying down in a lounge chair shape and sipped my coffee, listening to the rush of water over rocks. Only a few birds were awake. I hoped for a sighting. Anything.

And then I saw a big bird flying down over the creek, following its path, headed directly toward me. I knew it was one of the big ones.

I held really still until it was literally over my head. As I threw my head back quickly to get a glimpse of its underside, I must have scared the shit out of it, because it stopped in mid-air above me, obviously startled, and, with two flaps of it humungous wings, made a half-circle and looked at me for a moment like "prey?" Then, realizing my size, thought better of it and kept on its way.

There was no mistaking the white head on the big brown body. The eagle was my sighting and a symbol. Freedom.

We have the freedom to make the choices in our lives that will shape it. How often do we choose what feels right? How often do we choose from the heart, despite our circumstances, relationships, and fears? How often do we make our own choices, no matter what others will think? How often do we choose to stay comfortable and safe to avoid what we think might happen if we take the risk? What, then, are we missing out on? Joy? Freedom? Love?

We could live our whole lives feeling safe, comfortable, and miserable. We could survive that way. That fear that stops us just looks like a wall of fire. When we make the leap and land on the other side, we realize that it was just a millimeter thick. That wall is worth examining a little closer, though.

The workshops that I'm blessed to be able to take have opened me up to the possibility of real healing, where you feel connected to a source that's so much bigger. They have encouraged me to follow my heart and my healing, and to find my voice. Each of them has been the greatest gift.

The people I've met there have been incredible. The John F. Barnes Myofascial Release courses have taught me to feel so I can teach my clients the same. They've taught me how to be afraid and feel anyway. They even taught me how to treat horses, which have become another passion of mine.

The joy I've felt since being around horses is hard to describe. Bliss would be a good word for it, just a step above joy. Working with horses is a mind-body event. If you lack awareness around them, you will pay. They demand your presence, they call your bluff, and they are amazing healing creatures.

Just to be able to feel a horse's nose can make your day. My daughter began her love of riding when we signed her up for a horseback riding summer camp. After that, we decided to sign her up for riding lessons, and she has been going once a week since.

Before this time, Danielle could not pick any one particular activity that she wanted to stick with. She tried dance for half a year and then quit. She played on the soccer team for one semester and then quit. When asked what she wanted to try, she would say, "I don't know."

Horseback riding was the first time she really wanted to do something. It didn't hurt that I've loved horses since I was a kid. I have been dabbling alongside of her, with a few lessons and a few trail rides, since she started lessons.

I love bringing her to the barn and being around the horses. The property of the barn begins when we make the right turn off the main road, and it is lined with fences for acres. We watch the horses grazing and sometimes rolling or frolicking in the fields, and it's awesome. We see if we can pick out some of the horses we know without their usual name tags.

When we enter the huge stables, the smell of the hay and the animals fills up my nose and makes me smile. As you walk down the row, there are about fifteen stalls on either side. I know some of you would be holding your noses at this point, but it's the opposite for me. I breathe deeper.

One day, Dani and I made our usual walk down the aisle with a bag of carrots, and we noticed that the staff was bringing in big bales of hay and buckets of mash. Feeding time!

All of a sudden, several horses started to neigh at the same time, filling our ears with a sound that vibrated right down to our toes. I had goosebumps, it was so magnificent. I wasn't thinking about anything else in that wonderful moment.

I really enjoy riding because, very much like Tae Kwon Do (and maybe even a little more so), you have to stay present. In this case, it's dangerous to be unfocused. Losing focus for even one second when you're around a horse might mean that you get hurt.

My daughter learned this the hard way one day when we were standing with Penne (her horse for the day) waiting for the lesson to start. She was holding his reins but had her back to the horse and was standing too close, not paying attention to him.

The horses were all fidgety that day because it was hot, and hot means flies. Horses don't like flies. Penne was stomping to get the flies off his legs, and Dani's foot ended up right underneath one of those stomps.

With tears in her eyes, she got up on that horse for her lesson that day. I was surprised; I thought we would be going home instead. But she got up and rode, and she rode well, as usual.

Very little deters my daughter when she's passionate about something. Sound familiar?

At the time of this new edition, it's seven years later. My daughter has her learner's permit and is very passionate about learning how to drive. She has envisioned the car she wants and has been adamant about her practice hours. No longer riding horses but still as determined, she got back in the car this week after having an accident.

And even though the accident wasn't her fault—maybe especially because it wasn't—she was afraid. Sometimes life doesn't feel like it's in your control. And whether it's a horse stomping on your foot or someone running into your car...we have to be brave, don't we?

The continued pursuit of our passionate dreams requires courage and persistence, no matter what life throws our way.

The following description is about the weekend I got to combine two of my passions, horses and physical therapy.

I was lucky enough to be able to attend a class called *Equine Myofascial Release*, given by Cathy Covell, who is a John Barnes Myofascial Release (JB/MFR) physical therapist in Indiana. Myofascial release is a hands-on treatment technique used to release restrictions in the body and is one of the best whole-body assessment and treatment techniques I've learned as a physical therapist. (Please visit www.myofascialrelease.com and read more if interested.)

My story today is about an amazing experience I had learning about horses and how to treat them using this technique.

My friends Phil and Ann and I travelled to Delaware on Friday night, arriving at the Best Western of Smyrna, Delaware, at 11 p.m., so off to bed we went. The next day, we made the trek over to The Whispering Meadows Stables, which was in Clayton, Delaware, about ten minutes away from the hotel. It was a large farm with three house-like buildings on it and a big stable with many horses.

I learned later that the farm had been purchased by a couple about five years previously and that Steve, one of the owners, had given up his day job as a lawyer to run the farm. The farm is located near a place called Dover Downs, which is a big race track, and several of the horses were retired race horses. They were fabulous, big, muscular, beautiful animals, and we were about to learn how to treat them!

We arrived and found a little room where our instructor was setting up. She lectured to us for about two hours that first morning about horses, myofascial release, horse anatomy, and safety. The rest of Saturday and Sunday was spent with our hands on the horses. There were fourteen students there, a combination of massage and physical therapists and not any "horse" people.

Each pair of students had a horse. During the day, we would switch both horse and human partners for variety. Some of the horses were old, some young, some were retired from the track, and one came all the way from New Zealand. We had all the boys first, then in the afternoon, all the ladies.

When one group heard the other group moving through the stables, there would be all sorts of wonderful commotion. The mares would paw at the ground and whinny, and some would "squirt," as our instructor called it, because they were in heat. We met Meagan, Cinnamon, No More Rain, Kailua, Reese, and many others.

We were taught several of the techniques as our instructor, Cathy, demonstrated on one of the horses while we watched. Then we were asked to close our eyes, take a deep breath, open our eyes, and see what horse we were drawn to. They were all tied in the alleyway of the stables, butts out.

The first horse I treated was called No More Rain, and she was a horse they told us was mean but was really a softy. I had a great partner, Wayne, a massage therapist from Delaware.

As we practiced the first technique, a transverse plane release, I started to cry. A huge sense of gratitude washed over me. I thought, *I can feel this stuff.*

It's not like I didn't already know I could feel a tissue release under my hands. I'd been doing it for fifteen years. But the horse was telling me, *You can feel this, all you have to do is get quiet and grounded.*

I felt a wave of sadness for the abuse that the animal may have been through in the past, and then I was awestricken at the healing it was doing, without judgement, without the noisy chatter, without having to analyze it or figure it out.

Horses can't speak to you, but they do communicate. It's up to us to listen—*really* listen—so the healing can happen. They say the horse is treating you while you are treating the horse. I know what they are talking about now. I left that morning with a sense of confidence, of rightness, and of truth: that I could trust myself, and what I feel. It was a gift beyond words.

We went through that day and the next practicing new techniques and watched the horses go from fidgeting and pawing and being noisy to literally falling asleep. Really!

My partner and I worked on Cinnamon the second day. Her owner was standing by observing the group. As we rotated her at the withers (the place just above where the saddle goes on the spine), her head got lower, and lower, and lower, her eyes eventually drooping and closing.

Our instructor asked the horse's owner, "Have you ever seen your horse like this?" And the owner laughed (like "are you kidding?") and said, "No, never." What an amazing confirmation it was to hear her say that, and to know that what we'd learned in two days could positively affect a 1500-pound animal. It felt like a miracle.

Toward the end of Sunday, we were supposed to practice the tail-pull technique. Yes, it's exactly what you think it is.

The main therapist at that point was to take the upper part of the horse's tail, about a foot down from where it connects to the animal, and gently lean back, like they are water skiing. We held this position for several minutes, and then the second therapist gently released the horse from the base of its neck, elongating in the other direction. Imagine!

The whole spine was being stretched and elongated from head to tail. How wonderful this must feel for the horse, to have someone listening, following, and helping them release a back that has had to carry who knows how many pounds, run who knows how many races, and suffer who knows what abuse.

Every horse in that stall was quiet during the tail pull. Nobody got kicked. In fact, as I looked around, most horse's heads were lowering, eyes closing. You really had to see it to believe it.

What this taught me about my practice with humans is that I should be clearer, softer, lighter, and more present in the moment. That if I can do that, they will have an easier chance to heal. I learned that the patient has to do the healing, and that it's my job to be a good facilitator. I learned that to push or force won't get you anywhere with a horse, and probably not very far with people either. I learned that to be connected is the key. And that connection I'm talking about is bigger than we realize; it's through every living creature. It is God. It is spirit. It is love at its roots.

Journal entry June 18, 2010:

Five days post pretest. The salt pills worked well…no cramping! In fact, I think they boosted my energy as well. I had good sparring energy, good board-breaking energy. I can't believe I broke three boards on my first try, thanks to the awesome holding by David and Diego. It was very nice to watch Madoka and Alex get their black belts. We set Jonathan's next test for Thursday at 7:30 p.m.

Journal entry June 24, 2010:

Jonathan completed his second pretest tonight. He tested alone. He asked me to practice forms with him, so we did it three times today. His dad came to the test. After we got home and the kids were asleep, my husband said to me, "He wasn't good."

He wasn't good? Those words make me want to cry. No matter what, I'm always going to be okay with the kids doing their best. I will always assume they're trying their best. He was awesome. Perfect.

I believe some of us spend our whole lives striving for perfection, whatever that is. Striving to achieve more, be excellent, get all A's. Then we make our kids be perfect. Well, we try to make them believe that that's the goal, and the cycle starts all over again. They become a reflection of our perfection.

I believe living with passion and following your passions is a perfect expression of who we really are. I don't think perfection has anything to do with a goal we should strive for.

Imagine that how we are right this moment, with all of our imperfections, problems, mistakes, and failures, is perfect. We need a new definition of perfection, my friends. The one we currently have was determined by everyone else but ourselves. We are whole and perfect just as we are.

In the next chapter, I explore my voice and reflect on the healing journey that helped me get it back. Turns out the Perfect Good Girl in me thought, for a long time, that expressing herself would make her unworthy. Turns out that was bullshit.

Are you pursuing your passions? Why or why not? How could you add more passion and joy to your life today?

Use these pages to record your thoughts about the questions at the beginning and end of this chapter...

Voice

A t what times in your life have you felt like you had a voice? When was it taken away?

I started facing the fear of speaking up in 2010. I needed my voice back. I could no longer live with the way not being able to speak my truth made me feel inside. The cost was too high. My amazing friend Phil encouraged me, for about a year, to look into something called the Landmark Forum. Many people have criticized this program for its cult-like feel, but I believe it helped me get my voice back.

First, a sign. Yes, I believe in signs.

Journal entry July 13, 2010

A week ago Monday, I woke up and let the dogs outside to pee as usual. A couple minutes later, I heard Reina barking her head off and went to the window to investigate. She was looking at the ground and barking. I went out to see what it was and, low and behold, there was a turtle in our yard! I named him Herman. I thought it was lucky to find him in our yard, even for a short period (he was gone by lunch time), so I emailed Robin to get her thoughts.

Robin emailed me back to say, "That is good luck!"

We have lived here for over twelve years and have never seen a turtle.

Fast forward to last night in Tae Kwon Do class. The first one ready to spar, as usual, I'm sitting on the balance beam waiting, staring down at the headgear in my hands, the helmet I've owned for four years, and notice that on the back of it right below where I wrote my initials is a picture of a turtle along with the words "Long Life Products." How many times have I looked at the back of my helmet? A thousand? None? I never noticed the turtle. I smiled a big smile and wished I had someone to tell. I couldn't believe it.

Then Master H. calls me out to spar with him. I get a heel bone in the meaty part of my right calf. Limping off, I have to stop. Off to the side, stretching, limping, the tears begin to fall. I'm tired, they say.

I can barely gather myself. Deep breath, stop the flow, back in line to spar with one leg, finish class. And the tears flow out the door. I'm not done, they say. All the way home, they fall. Sitting in front of my house in the car, they are falling. Emailing Robin, they fall, and in the house hiding from everyone, they fall harder. My family notices, but they go to sleep. Can't speak.

Sometimes I don't know what the tears are about, only that they need to fall. I have guessed that years of not speaking up, speaking my truth, or speaking from my heart have gathered into a well of tears that leak out when the well is full. I try not to question it too much anymore.

The breakthrough I had during The Forum became the first topic of my pretest number three essay for the following January, but I never turned that essay in to Master Holloway. I was still afraid to tell the world, even when it was one of the best things I'd ever done.

Journal entry October 17, 2010:

So, now I can talk to my dad. Without the heavy baggage of resentment. I can start to separate myself from the past so that I can speak from my heart. Whenever I need or want to. I have to defend my kids and protect myself and them, but now I can. I'm also starting to be able to talk to my husband about it. And I think I will be able to talk to most anyone.

So, here is that essay.

Pretest Three Essay–first attempt, never turned in.

Back in October, I attended a workshop called The Landmark Forum. It was an intense three-and-a-half-day workshop that ultimately transformed my life by giving me the tools to be able to talk to people.

I now view life, and especially relationships, in a new way. I experienced a dramatic breakthrough in my relationship with my dad while attending.

Before the Forum, I had what you might call an obligatory relationship with my dad. I did not enjoy his company much, my family did not enjoy him, and I could not feel or express love in that relationship.

What I realized in this amazing three days was that there had been a time in my young life with my dad when, because of the way he treated my sister and I, I decided that he hated me. The more amazing thing was I realized I'd spent the last 34 years of my life believing it and living my story about it. I had a 34-year-old complaint and a way of being around my dad that cost me a lot of love.

The real breakthrough came on day two of the workshop, when our homework was to call someone with whom we felt "incomplete." I called my dad in California, and he answered. Gulp.

I choked out something like, "Dad, I've been taking this class this weekend, and I'm learning a lot of new things. I just wanted to tell you that I have been making you wrong for thirty-four years, and that I'm sorry, and I love you."

Another "gulp."

My amazing dad who, you will remember, I thought for the last thirty-four years hated me, said, "I love you, too." He stepped up to the plate, opened his arms wide, and just accepted me. I then experienced, while standing there in the parking lot of the workshop with my cell phone on my ear, a very light feeling, as if a 34-year-old weight had lifted.

My dad got on a plane the next day to come out to the East

Coast to be with me for the visitor night of the Forum, and sat by my side. We spent the two days of his visit talking about life and golf and Tae Kwon Do and the kids, and for the first time in a long time, I enjoyed being there with him. It felt softer.

Now, three months later, I call my dad to say hi because I genuinely want to, because I love him. That has never been easy for me.

Since the Forum, my life and relationships continue to open. I feel a freedom, power, and self-expression I didn't have before. I have a confidence to act even when I'm afraid.

Other relationships with significant people in my life are getting easier and finally working. There's a certain ease in relating to others now, even when there are problems. I see myself dealing effectively with changes, and even more so being able to shape my future.

When I started in my Tae Kwon Do journey four-and-a-half years ago, I feel like I was beginning to learn how to be a warrior, how to use my body and mind in a way that enhanced my abilities, my focus, and my life. I remember in my first class, Ms. M was teaching me a side kick, and I loved every minute of that class, felt an instant "Yes, this is it!" feeling about it, but I had no way of knowing the amazing journey that was before me. That the skills, confidence, and courage I was learning would serve me later.

To be able to take a class like The Forum, get the transformation required to act despite my fear, and focus my mind enough so the fear doesn't take over and prevent me from acting feels priceless.

The Tae Kwon Do classes, tests, and tournaments all prepared me to be able to do this. Now that I know what I know and have gained the particular insights I've gained from this extraordinary education, there are no longer any excuses that could get in the way of my dreams. Nothing except my own fear can get in the way.

So here goes...

I think you, Master M, and I should get together and open up a Gentle East satellite in Bethesda. Master M should manage it, and I will help teach classes. This studio could also have a "wellness" aspect.

I could offer workshops in stretching, injury prevention, muscle balance, body awareness, etc...every month. My bigger dream (why not get big here) is to own a healing/fitness center that is big enough to house Gentle East classes in the evenings, where someone could come for physical therapy, massage, acupuncture, etc. by day and take classes and workshops by night.

I have always had the pleasure of saying that I love my job, that it, as a part of my life, feels seamless, not really like a job. I've had a passion for Tae Kwon Do since the beginning, and I know I can incorporate it into my "work." When you can go to work and it doesn't feel like you are going to work, wow! How can you beat that?

Okay, it's now out there in black and white, and I can't take it back. You know the dream. Thanks for listening.

Actualizing a dream takes a lot more than thinking it up. To have excellence in my life as a possibility means that excellence has to be a way of being, beginning with what is in my life, but transcending that to generate new possibilities.

Excellence means that I'm being in life, right now, intending for the fulfillment of a possibility. It's an ongoing state of being, a moment-by-moment practice. Being fully present in the moment and living that moment with an intention of fulfilling a dream.

It's really easy to have many wishes, dreams, and goals, to the point of writing them down and piecing out the steps. I've spent many years and used a lot of paper doing that. The hard part is living in each moment of life with the intention to fulfill them. Speaking them, sharing them, shouting them to anyone who will listen. Continually creating. Not striving, not comparing, not trying to overcome the past or guess the future. Taking action!

There have been many a goal created only to disappear soon after. The difference between making them and realizing them is how you're being in the now and whether or not you're living with integrity in each moment and sharing your dreams out loud.

I was a black belt in my mind on that first day of class four-and-a-half years ago. I've been talking about it ever since. This journey, once you choose to take it, is more like layers being uncovered. The core is black, covered by red, blue, green, yellow, and white. Some people strive for the black, but the secret is, they already had it in the first place. Living it in this moment is the key to uncovering it.

Re-reading this essay seven years later while writing this book's new edition is so interesting. I'm not living the dream in this essay. Maybe, then, that's why I never shared it. Hmm.

And, for perspective, some days, I just do the laundry and complain about it.

The following poem came out of my participation in this same Forum workshop. I came out of the intense weekend more *me*. With more voice. With less fear. With tools to communicate with people. The hard people.

Thanks, Randy. Not only did I write this poem, I stood up at the microphone and read it to my classmates one night with sweaty palms and my heart feeling like it would explode. Yikes!

Who New

I wait for a beginning
a new possibility
that I made space for
when what I was blind to
became known
That instant in time
became light and free
the moment I saw
what I made things to mean.
My rackets aren't me
What would grow from that space
I couldn't have guessed.
Power.
Freedom.
Pure spirit self-expressed.
I am not more or different or changed
like my whole life
trying to mend
but bigger, more whole, from the heart

a transformation in the end.
And now I know with ease
when my power, freedom, and peace
are being taken from me
and all I have to do
it seems...
Is notice
and remember my oath.
The one I made to myself and the world
for my life and yours
of courage, integrity, and love
Letting my actions and words
speak my view
listening to yours too
I find a new voice and a new ear
and I think I like it here.
I'm thinking so will you.

Journal entry January 30, 2011

Had my third pretest yesterday after a long week of no school and the flu. My husband in Seattle until Thursday night missed the snow and the shoveling. We experienced something called thunder snow, like a blue and orange light show in the clouds. I never heard any thunder.

We had a good, short test. Seemed easy. Oh, did I actually just say that out loud? We had eighteen testers. Wonder what the record is. I woke up nervous yesterday morning, couldn't help it, couldn't shake it, but as soon as we started, I was fine.

Combo kicks—Master Lindeire—I was thinking, aren't there supposed to be eight kicks in a combo? And, why is he hollering like that? Oh my...Master H. had his number and made him do kick combos, I don't know, like ten more times. Kicked his butt.

I love Tae Kwon Do.

I want to start my business plan for Tae Kwon Do classes at our center. And I feel so funny about it all. No confidence. Fear. Fear of not being good enough.

I was sick with the flu when I wrote the Pretest Three Essay. I think I was probably a little crazy that week. When I read the essay again, I think I was definitely a little crazy.

I was so worried about being perfect. It wasn't worth the worry.

The real Pretest Three Essay January 29, 2011

I'm having trouble with this essay. This is my second attempt. I love this part of the test, love to write, but I am having trouble with this one. Mostly because I want it to be perfect. So because I have this idea about what perfect should be, the stuff that comes out sounds stupid, not good enough, not worthy.

I want it to be perfect, from the part of me that is real, the authentic me. The me that wants to write about some amazing thing, some incredible insight or lesson I have learned, something perfect, is not the real me. It comes from a false place of striving and comparing and competing and is based on the past.

I want to write from this moment, give you the real me. Unfortunately, the real present moment me has a cold, is planted on the couch in flannel pajamas reaching for the Kleenex every five seconds. No amazing thing, insight, lesson. Just a red nose. So I search my mind for something brighter. Hannah Montana on the TV is slightly distracting, and so is my scratchy throat.

I'm thinking about talking with Giselle in class the other day, about her struggle with testing because she wants so badly to "nail it." Her words. And the debate going on inside her head about her being ready enough, or having it be perfect.

I'm thinking about my girlfriend whose son does Tae Kwon Do but has not competed in a tournament yet because she's afraid he'll be disappointed if he doesn't win. "I just don't think he is ready," she says to me.

I think there are a lot of people who are afraid of failure, afraid of disappointment, afraid of getting hurt, afraid they aren't good enough/in shape enough, just plain afraid. Fear can be paralyzing. And fear can be motivating. What if we taught our children—and ourselves, for that matter—to take fear on?

I loved what you said to the kids at the test about fear, that if you saw they were afraid, then you would make them take it on or else that fear would never get out of the way. The problem with running away from the fear, or waiting for a better time to act, is that in the meantime, the fear is still in the way. The trick to fear is to take action in spite of it. This is called courage.

I recently had the experience of being able to redefine the meaning of excellence as it relates to my life. The instructor of the Landmark Seminar told us that any current definition of the word was based on a story we made up in our minds, based on the past or the future.

The light bulb went off for me when he had us make a list of all of the things that excellence has meant up until now: being perfect, being better than someone else, getting straight A's, winning the game, looking perfect, having the right friends/mate/job/life, being able to have or do _____ (fill in the blank with anything you don't have now but want for your future).

I realized that everything on my list was a story I'd made up. None of it was what actually happened. It was all based on past or future, none of it present-moment based, none of it reality. I was then left with nothing.

I had the feeling that everything I'd been striving for all my life was based on a made-up story. A big, blank nothing space. And that is exactly where he wanted us to be, because the only way to have the space to create something new is to start with a clear, open space, a space for a new possibility.

The idea that he left us with was to show up in life, in the moment, with an intention to fulfill a possibility. The possibilities are ours to create. But once we create them, it's our responsibility to live in the moment, from our commitment to them, with an intention to fulfill them. The problem with living in your head is that the crap in there is all a story, constantly being made up as you go and getting in the way a lot.

The only way to have excellence as a possibility in life is to stop striving, stop comparing, stop living in the past or the future. Now is the moment where you have the power and the freedom to be new.

Back to being perfect...I have finally realized there's no such thing. So I'm sitting on my couch with this cold, knowing that I don't feel 100 percent and that I haven't been able to do the extra training I wanted to do for this test coming up, thinking that I will not feel well enough for it to perform up to perfect standards (whose perfect standard?).

And all this time I spend in my head about the "what if's" just makes me more nervous and anxious. Meanwhile, at this moment, I have a stuffy nose and a cough, that is all, and I have six days to rest, feel better, practice my moves, and study.

Who knows how Saturday will go? But one thing I know for sure: I would be much more disappointed if I didn't participate, even if I don't feel 100 percent, because being there with the friends I've made; doing this incredible thing together, something you think you might not be able to do; facing your fear and overcoming it, all with the support of my teachers and friends, is priceless.

I know Giselle will be there. I know she knows what I'm talking about, even though she hasn't experienced it yet. As for my girl-friend and her son, I hope he has the opportunity to compete soon and have the feeling of being part of something bigger, win or lose, trophy or no trophy.

Ultimately, I'm living with the possibility that I can teach this, that I'm teaching this by example in my life, that there will be someone watching me and thinking, I can do that, too. What a gift it is to be able to help people face their fears with action, to watch them overcome and triumph. So, to those who are waiting to be perfect, to be ready, to be happy, to have or be enough, I suggest you stop waiting and start living. Make the most of the moment, face a fear with action, redefine your life, create a new possibility, and live like you intend to fulfill it. It is way more fun that way.

About six hours after writing the above part of this essay, I came down with the flu. The gross stomach kind. I can count on one hand the number of times I've had this kind of flu in my whole life, and I still have fingers left over when I'm done counting.

In the last twenty-four hours, my mind has gone slightly crazy. I couldn't come to class on Monday night, the last good workout I wanted to give myself before the test, and who knew if I'd make it on Thursday? Would I be okay for the test, and even if I thought I would be okay, what if I tried and wasn't okay?

I played the serious "what if" game for those twenty-four hours. Torture. Discipline the mind, I heard in my head. So I tried, but mostly I slept, pulled myself out of bed a couple times to make sure the kids weren't killing each other (they had Monday off of school and we had fun things planned originally), and then went back to bed, literally aching from head to toe.

I woke up today feeling much better, saw my miracle worker acupuncturist, and spent a quiet day with some "what if" moments still lingering but put on The Karate Kid and decided to motivate myself. Damn it, if a twelve-year-old can win the match with a broken leg and no sparring gear, then I can do this! Heck, I've experienced childbirth—twice! What is wrong with me?

So I write tonight with an even newer vision of excellence. One that includes minimizing the "what if " game in my mind as much as possible, making space for possibility (that this could be an awesome test), practicing the things I can, leaving the rest to the preparation I already have done, and taking action even with fear. Perfect. For now.

Forgive the ongoing nature of this essay, for it has become a lifeline this week. And so here I am on the fourth day since I started writing, doing a better job of choosing a still mind and feeling slightly better physically. I have gained much knowledge in Korean history, including an interesting bit about Hwarang. What I learned is that Hwarang means "flower knight" (made me think of the name Gentle East), and these "knights" were an elite group of male youth who were greatly influenced by Buddhism and Taoism.

But the more interesting tidbit from the Samguk sagi (historical record of the three kingdoms of Korea) and the Samguk yusa (collection of legends, folktales and historical accounts) was that there was also a group called the wonhwa, or "original flowers," who were a group of females said to precede the Hwarang.

Women played a larger prominent social role than men in pre-Confucianism Korea, especially in Silla, which had three reining queens in its history. But who knows if they were allowed to practice things like Tae Kwon Do. I found it amusing, though, to find any information on women, and I wondered what it would have been like during that time in the world. I think maybe for the next competition, I'll make up a creative form and call it wonhwa.

Okay, I have decided to hit "print" for the last time and not be afraid of this being perfect. What it was, was me. Whole and complete in this moment.

This is a letter to family about The Captain's Cup Challenge 2010:

Hi everyone!

Jonathan and I had a great day at our Tae Kwon Do tournament yesterday. We were there bright and early to help our teachers set up the venue. Danielle was a volunteer and helped at one of the sign-in tables all morning.

The competition started at 10:00 a.m., and by then the gym was packed! There were over 200 competitors signed up, which may have been a record for Master Holloway. There was not a free spot in the bleachers, and it made for an exciting time. We gathered all of our classmates for an excellent warm-up and headed for the gym.

The day opened with Traditional Forms, then Creative Forms, then Family Forms (Jonathan and I). They announced our category over the loud speaker, and we went over to the staging area to wait.

When it was time to put us into groups, the organizers were debating how to proceed, because it looked to be uneven. I suggested, with Jonathan's approval, that they go ahead and put us in the black belt group. What was I thinking?

Well, as I told Jonathan, we were there to have fun, going up against black belts was a great experience, and we were at least going to get a bronze out of it. To my surprise, he said, "Sure, Mom."

Our competition was two teams of brothers, one team younger, and the other team was Victor and Steven from Gentle East. I won't say our performance was flawless, but close! And we won a silver medal in Family Forms. The younger brothers won the gold.

Now it was board-breaking time (my favorite). We had practiced our board-breaking routines in class by going over the choreography with people pretending to be holding boards up.

Today, we would have two tries for each station; if you can't break the board after two tries, then you move on to the next board. Jonathan and I had each come up with a routine that had four board-breaking stations (the max allowed).

Jonathan was up first and had four other competitors in his category, three other red belts and one black belt. His dad and I each held a board for him. He missed the first board, supposed to be a back kick, but broke the other three boards with a back kick, an axe kick, and a side kick.

He won a silver medal in this competition! His board breaking is getting better each year, and I'm noticing his confidence and strength grow each time he competes.

Then it was time for me. My first kick was supposed to be a side kick, and for the first time I was trying it with my left leg. Well, I missed twice. I broke the next three boards with a side kick, a jump turning kick (a first try), and a reverse turning kick with my left leg (another first try).

Then I could hear Master Holloway saying, "Come break this board!" He was at the first station where I had missed, helping the other board holder so now I had two people holding that board. Again I heard him say, "Come break this board!" So I did! I won a gold in board breaking (for the first time!) in that competition against three other women.

It was time for lunch at this point, so we all had a short break while we geared up for an afternoon of sparring. The opening ceremonies started after lunch. They had all the competitors come into the middle of the gym and line up by school.

This was the biggest showing for Gentle East I had seen, with our students taking up two full lines in the gym. It was so great to see that, and I felt proud to be a part of it. Master Holloway welcomed everyone, we sang the national anthem, and he introduced many of the people that he had there with him, including his teacher!

At that point, the entire gym stood up and bowed. That was a goosebumps moment. There were also nine international-level referees present, including one man from Kenya!

In these types of tournaments, you are lucky if you have one international referee. During that ceremony, it was evident that we were part of something special, a love for this sport and a love for Master Holloway. We are so lucky to be a part of the Gentle East school.

This is the time when your adrenaline starts to build. We are nervous and excited. We are being grouped together and matched up with our competitors and are silently sizing up our competition.

The matches start with the youngest age category, so there's a fair amount of waiting-while-nervous happening. The gym is filled with cheering, shouting, screaming, kihaps (yells), and general craziness.

Later, on the ride home, Jonathan and I would talk about how, in a gym full of people and intense noise, you could easily hear the voice of your loved one coaching you from the sidelines. Reminded me of March of the Penguins.

There were four boys in Jonathan's group. He won his first match in overtime, 1 to 0. He was tough, didn't back down, and got the point to win the match. That meant that he had to fight a second match for the championship. In the second match, it was 0 to 0 for three quarters of the match. Jonathan scored at that point and won the match 1 to 0! This was Jonathan's first gold medal in sparring.

When it was time for me to spar, it was late in a very long day, as the 33-and-up category goes last. That's a lot of waiting-while-nervous! There were six people in our group: a red stripe, three red belts, including me, and two black belts. We ranged in age from 30's to 50's, but at that point, you just want someone to spar against, so we all agreed to have one big match.

I was paired with my classmate Lori for the first round and won 7 to 0. In sparring, there's something called a seven-point gap, so if you reach seven points without the other person scoring, you automatically win the match and the time stops.

Lori did a fantastic job in the match, which was her first in a tournament, and I was grateful to get to spar with her. I then had to go up against the winner of the other match, who ended up being a 38-year-old black belt. I lost 8 to 4 and was extremely proud to have scored 4 points against a black belt and win a silver medal in sparring.

The tournament was an amazing way to bring a year of hard work together and see the results. I am incredibly proud of Jonathan and, well, of myself too, for hanging in there, working hard, practicing consistently, and having the courage to compete. Thanks to our teachers, Master McDermott, Master Hathway, and Master Holloway for their skills, patience, and love of the sport. And thanks to all of you who sent us good luck vibes; they worked!

Love, Laura

It was in September of the same year that I decided to start writing my blog, which began as healing stories and some Tae Kwon Do stories but was mainly a work blog. It morphed into Living, Healing and Tae Kwon Do, as an expression of my passions in life, to include all of them, not just my day job. It gave me a voice and allowed my writing to be read, shared, and enjoyed by someone else besides me.

Some people look at me and laugh when I tell them that finding my voice and expressing my true self is my healing path. They already see the confident, outgoing, expressive parts of me, the parts that teach them all about their bodies and how to recover from an injury. In some corners of my life, I feel grounded in confident expression. In others, I shrivel into a 3-year-old.

I laughed out loud one day when the mom of one of Dani's new friends, surprised in finding out I was a physical therapist, said, "Oh! I thought you must be in some kind of sales, you're so outgoing!" Oh my God, if she only knew.

The fear is old, early conditioned fear. I'm finally recognizing it for what it is. The recognition itself makes space for a new opportunity, for making a new choice, to not be afraid to speak. When I feel like a scared 3-year-old, I remember what it is now. I put my 43-year-old arm around the inner 3-year-old and say, "We can do this." And it works most of the time. At least I am able to do something or say something instead of hide.

When I was three and had to have my tonsils out, the trauma of that experience—and many, many traumatic medical experiences after that—instilled a fear inside of me.

I could not express myself except to scream for my mom. Even then, nobody listened. In fact, they just pulled me away as I screamed, stuck my arms with big needles, and knocked me out with some gross-smelling gas.

I was screaming for my life, and nobody listened. I didn't matter, nobody was coming to save me. Harsh, I know. But to a 3-year-old, it is life or death.

Unfortunately, it was male doctors who didn't listen. Back then, doctors had some kind of Godlike quality, and people just obeyed without questioning or wondering if there was another way. There was no alternative option.

They told you what you needed, and you said okay. They were supposed to know what they were talking about, and you weren't supposed to question them. Unfortunately, the way I felt about my father at the time was probably very similar.

I have very little memory of the following seven ear operations I had. I do remember the final ear drum reconstruction (as an adult) and the thumb ligament reconstruction (also as an adult). But that does not make those last two any less traumatic.

I still had absolutely no real voice in those situations. I was just relying on these people to fix me and following their orders, barely surviving the severe needle phobia I was left with and not knowing how to tell people I was deathly afraid.

So, for most of my adult life, I felt three years old again when I had to interact with a male authority figure, especially a doctor, and always with my dad.

I would never defend myself, never really speak up, never even give my opinion, even when it had to do with my own body and feelings. I didn't even know how to tell people I was afraid.

Wow, if I couldn't do it, there was surely nobody else who would. So I lived somewhat shriveled, invisible, without much confidence, and with a large amount of fear for a really long time. Even in my relationship with my husband, most of my thoughts, opinions, concerns, and even joys stayed inside my little head for nobody to understand but me.

By far, the most difficult thing for me now as an adult is being sick. I panic. I go into immediate thinking overdrive at the first sign of a sniffle.

My mind starts to ask a lot of questions: *What if I can't work? What if the kids get sick? Is it going to take me forever to get rid of it? What if I can't work out? What if I can't test? What if I have to take another antibiotic?*

Holy shit.

The "what if" game is torture. I have slowly—very slowly— dropped the panic reaction to my illnesses, taken them for what they are (a frickin' head cold), and practiced being sick. Thanks, Robin.

The essay for my third pretest was an all-out written version of that kind of panic. Being sick mattered in a different way this time. It meant I was going to miss out on a peak performance Tae Kwon Do experience. I really do put a lot of pressure on myself.

I will never forget part of Master Holloway's speech at the end of that test (he knew I had been really sick with the flu). He casually added into his usual motivating words that it wouldn't matter how sick Master M or Master Hathway were, that they would show up anyway in the pure spirit of competition.

There was no way they would let the other get ahead in rank by not showing up just because they were sick. I sat on the floor at the end of that test and smiled as I looked up to hear his words more clearly. I have to tell you, Master Holloway, how much those couple of sentences helped me that day. I healed a little bit in that moment.

Journal entry May 29, 2011

Voice. Something is clicking from last week. My daughter has a voice. How can I make sure she keeps it? As a kid, your voice is annoying, misbehaving, aggravating, out of control. So we suppress it, control it, stop it, try to make her think it is wrong. It is a wonder we ever grow up and function, really.

Me at age 43, so afraid to have a voice. So afraid I can't find it when I need it. So late in life finding a way to fight, silently, with my body. A way to express with no words at all. Saying, "See, I can fight," "I have something to say," "I am good." Expressing without speaking.

If we only exist as our spoken word, then what is this kind of expression, and why is it important? We only exist in relationship to others, so that they can know who we are with our spoken word. "I am." A warrior. For joy.

Warrior for Joy

I knew I was a warrior when:
I beat a six-foot-tall man in a Tae Kwon Do sparring match.
I rode a horse fast for the first time and thought, "I have done this before."
I survived a surgeon cutting a four-inch incision in my arm while I was awake, feeling fight-or-flight but in a frozen state, like I would surely die.

I called my dad and let him know that I had let go.

Found my voice in spite of feeling nauseous.

I have figured out that there are two main triggers to my fear and lack of voice, the first of which is being sick (helpless) and the second is speaking to someone who I think might be angry about what I have to talk about.

To say that I'm non-confrontational is an understatement. Having a daughter who seems to be the opposite is a strange challenge. My husband argues that she needs discipline. I argue that I don't want to squash her voice and that we have to pick our battles.

There are many a day where I want to pull my hair out over the power struggle that's going on, and then I always remember where I came from and usually give in. Bad mommy. Not sure how I will pay for this later, but I probably will.

In 2010, I reconnected with an old friend of mine whom I'd worked with two jobs ago, in 1997. We were good work friends back then, enjoyed providing the physical therapy services that we did, and worked our jobs with laughter every day. After we each parted that job at different times for different reasons, we kept in touch and ended up having lunch once or twice per year.

The reconnect was my initiation during the time that my daughter started taking horseback riding lessons. My friend and her partner lived on a farm with horses, and horses were her partner's vocation. I had questions and emailed to say hi, what's up, what do you think about Dani starting to ride, what do we need to know?

I'm writing this now knowing how big the bigger picture turned out, and I have to chuckle. If I only knew I would get such an incredible opportunity to have a voice.

My friend invited the kids and I to come see the farm. The gals now had five horses, nine dogs, eighteen cats, and multiple chickens on more than ten acres a half mile from the river. It was heaven there. I dreamed of moving my family and living the country life. I dreamed hard.

We visited many times in a short amount of months, as many times as we could get away from our usual over-packed weekends. We looked at a property next door. I changed pre-arranged plans to get there. My friend and her partner welcomed me and my kids with open arms and a kindness that was extraordinary.

They were open, be-yourself-because-I-love-who-you-are kind of people. My friend and I talked a lot, fed and mucked the horses, and talked some more. Her partner was suffering from alcoholism. Mine from workaholism. We fell into a place with each other that felt comfortable and helpful and like deep friendship. We spent a lot of time together in those months talking about what love meant and how relationships got the way they got. Our friendship filled the hole that each of us had growing inside of us. We could be ourselves, no judgements.

Later, I would call myself blind and stupid. My friend's partner called one night to tell me that my friend had taken a bottle of pills to try to kill herself and was taken to the hospital.

I showed up at the hospital as soon as I could. No one else had come. No one else. I sat until there was a plan for her to go home. She was messed up. I had no clue how messed up. Had I done this? Why hadn't her partner come to see her or help her?

The time I spent in the hospital with my friend was surreal. She would later tell me she had no memory of that day. They say that sometimes we have to hit bottom before we can start to climb out again. This counted as the bottom.

I showed up at the farm a couple more times after that by myself to offer support. We talked some more about life. And then my friend tried to tell me how she really felt, about everything, her life, her job, and me. She showed up at my house. She tried to tell me she loved me and was overwhelmed by her emotions.

I tried to tell her she was still my friend and that I loved her and wanted her to be happy. We had a lengthy, uncomfortable debate about love versus friendship. It got really messy. Really difficult. Really awkward. And I couldn't speak.

I couldn't tell her the truth from a place in my heart that I thought wouldn't hurt her. I was a wimp. I asked her to go away and not talk to me. I judged her and rejected her. We haven't spoken since. More work to do.

In the meantime, I did begin to speak to my husband about everything. I opened up with nothing to lose. I tried to connect by letting him into my thoughts rather than walking around the house quietly, living inside my head.

I asked for his opinion. I told him little things I was thinking and some of the bigger things too. I did it even though I was afraid of what he would say and what he would think of me. I began to like the connection. It felt softer somehow.

Big picture. From the devastating loss of a good friend to reconnecting with my spouse. From complete loss of confidence to regaining strength and faith. There is no way I could have predicted the dots that I can now connect. The path was no fun at all. But it was necessary. More proof that I should not judge or reject the circumstances or people in my life just because they are uncomfortable or difficult. What are they trying to teach me? What's the opportunity? Can I recognize myself in that person and be kind?

When I showed up in Tae Kwon Do class this particular week, I was depressed, confused, and feeling fragile. Things were screaming on the inside, and I wanted them to shut up and go away. I showed up to exercise. Remember, it's my drug. Only this time, it didn't numb me out; it just accentuated my chaos.

Brett threw out a back kick that tagged me in the one-inch area of my back that isn't protected by the pads. It hurt. I kept going. Then he slammed me with another kick to the back where the prior year I'd been kicked hard enough to send me for an x-ray.

It knocked the breath and the confidence out of me, and the emotion couldn't be stuffed anymore. I managed to blurt out something about him being twice my weight and that he didn't need to try to knock me out. I was done.

Poor Diego had to listen to me sniffle and gasp next to him in line-up, even though I tried as hard as I could to stuff it. There was just no room left inside. The cost was too high.

I was forced to been seen, vulnerable and shaken. And it was okay, because I also had a sense that day in that room that the people in line had been there, and even if they hadn't, they were my friends. We would meet another new day to spar again. They held me that day without knowing that they were holding me. That is my Tae Kwon Do.

Journal entry May 14, 2011

Jonathan and I competed in the Maryland East Coast Open TKD Championship today. It was a hard tournament. Forms: Third place for both of us. Neither of us placed for boards. Jon had an awesome first sparring match, won 9 to 0, then second match lost 8 to 4. He really did a nice job, fought hard. I was so proud of him. It takes guts.

Journal entry May 29, 2011

My brave little girl will ride in her first show today. All dressed in her garb, pink and tan and black with a black velvet top.

She spoke to me about not winning...convinced. I spoke to her about her thoughts and keeping them positive, convinced she wasn't buying it. Then yesterday she began to write in her notebook, and I had a glance.

We just left for the movies, tomorrow I'm going to be in a horse show. I'm so excited! I can't wait. I am going to ride Tara. I think I will get first place! My mom thinks I will get first place too, because the older the horse is, the more chances you'll get to win first place! Before the movies we went to California Pizza Kitchen. Dad's not allowed to look until tomorrow. I will look pretty spiffy. I'll look like this: tan pants, a pink polo shirt, a helmet, a black helmet cover.

I'm not sure what I feel, but it's happy. A girl who will have an adventurous life, who will follow her passions, who will not be afraid to speak up.

Here is that theme showing up again in my journal.

Journal entry July 16, 2011

When Master M said "December," my heart sank. I was hoping for August or September. But we will live with December. We have no choice but to be okay with it. It's part of the journey. And the truth is that we need the time anyway. So, hopefully not right after the cruise and hopefully not right before Christmas. Maybe we can request a date now.

I got knocked down, blown into my world of reality, the not-so-bad one. And all of a sudden I should settle for what is here. I'm unsure but for a moment felt warm about it. Then hard. Then warm. Mostly unsure. Will have to be okay with living in the gap. Isn't it always a gap?

IAGF

My kids, who they are, what they are doing.
How Rocky (my blind dog) finds me no matter where I am.
Dog noises, cuddles, smiles, and tails.
Myself for wanting to be better at life.
Horses and how they take care of me.
Bird songs.
No longer inflated by praise or deflated by criticism.

My husband comes into the room while I'm on my computer writing, as I have been doing for the past week in all my spare moments, and asks, "Whacha doin'?"

"Writing," I say.

He stands there behind me, and I feel him reading my screen. I try not to squirm or slam the cover down on my laptop. Then he says, "You can't have it be just all journal entries."

I hear, *this is a terrible idea, you are stupid, why are you even trying to write a book, you don't know what you are doing.*

I know, I know. So I blurted out some reaction defending myself and left the room to fold more laundry.

It took me thirty minutes to come back into the room, where he had quickly moved on to watching *American Pickers,* and tell him what happens when I hear criticism.

I explain that it obliterates my self-confidence, but that I'm working on a better response. And he tries to defend himself. I interrupt and let him know that the purpose of telling him these things is not to bash him but to let him have a little window into my fragile brain.

I feel better for finding my voice. Last year, something like that would have festered for days before I pushed it so far down inside of me that I couldn't find or feel it anymore. Talk about it? Please! Too easy. I'd rather suppress the bad feeling and use up all my energy keeping it down so that I don't have to feel it or talk about it. NOT.

Nowadays, I'm weighing the cost of feeling crappy and holding onto that crap inside of me until I hurt against the cost of growing balls and saying something in the moment when I feel crappy.

The first choice has a higher cost. I've spent my whole life paying those dues. I have no choice but to figure this stuff out and speak. Even when I am afraid.

Miércoles!

I practice a dance now of listening to a person, noticing how I'm feeling as they are speaking, not judging my reaction or their words, and letting myself feel my words in response, if there need to be any words at all.

The dance. I like this dance. I control it most of the time from my grounded place. When I feel the anxious-up-in-my-head, scrunchy type of stress in response to someone's words, I know I need to listen first.

Which means listening to them without thinking of what I will say, and listening to my heart to find words. Sometimes there are none. Some people can't stand that. Well, I can sit with that too.

The dance I'm describing is not easy. It takes focus. Discipline. When I discipline my mind, my body always follows. Change your thoughts, slow your heart rate, decrease your blood pressure, release your muscle contractions, improve your blood flow. Yeah, it works like that.

The fear of speaking up is a feeling in your body. What would it take to feel the feeling and speak anyway?

Finding and expressing my voice has been the biggest healing journey of my life. In the next chapter, I'll talk about other important forms of healing and the idea of knowing there's healing to do in the first place.

Do you live in full self-expression? Where might you speak up to express your true self? How would that feel?

Use these pages to record your thoughts about the questions at the beginning and end of this chapter...

Healing

W*hat things in your life have you had to heal from? What still needs to be healed?*

Healing has come in many forms over the years, some physical, some mental, some emotional, some energetic. I'm lucky to know of these different ways to heal body, mind, and spirit and even luckier I get to teach these techniques.

I was ready for a healing adventure when I got ready to drive to Valley Forge, Pennsylvania, for some continuing education in 2011. For the first time, I was taking not one but two courses back to back and spending several days away from my home and family to reboot.

I've found that if I don't have time alone, I start to get cranky. I have to fit these trips into my schedule creatively so they don't coincide with my husband being away for work. For me, the mom, being away means a lot of organizing of the kids, their schedule of activities, the dogs (including medication for one of them), food, laundry, and who knows what else I am forgetting.

By the time I'm on my trip, I usually already feel tired and worried that I've forgotten something important, but I also feel some relief. I'm by myself at last, only responsible for me. This is a necessary thing. I have to remind myself every year that it's necessary, because I tend to let guilt get in the way of these kind of recharging trips.

Journal entry May 22, 2011

Transformation.

Three days of Myofascial Rebounding, one day of Cervico-Thoracic. Back in my room with a different body, one that is beautiful, nice to look at. Shifted, transformed. What was it that shifted?

Second day of C-T—after a long class, went for a walk with Iveta. A long walk. Kept walking, talking about life. And kept walking. A different body was walking. And a healing crisis in the midst of my walk/talk.

An old familiar symptom of the old me body. Dropping out, painful, hold myself kind of ache. But just from a walk, never before from just a walk. How could it be? What was happening? Was I destabilized? Was that God (HA! Mistype—good)?

Walked and talked some more. Rested. I never could rest before. Never could say, "Okay, I need to rest." Always pushing on, striving, running, straining. Never listening, feeling, resting. So we sat on the grass and talked some more, and I rested my core. Let it rest. You have time. I had to get back to the car, and part of me wondered if I would have to ask Iveta to take my car keys, go find the car, and come for me. Part of me wondered if I would make it.

We walked again, and I was okay. And this morning I'm fine. What the hell? Am I tight again? Did my body reorganize and remain shifted? Yes. I feel open, lighter, less effortful. My core is light, not strained. And it feels balanced. It might need more rest. I can do that. I can ask for that. It is only just what I need. And that is important. My voice.

What adventures will be coming, I can't wait to see.

This journal entry is about another one of those kinds of continuing education courses. I was feeling a shift in myself physically and mentally, and the class felt like it boosted me into some kind of higher level of intensity of all of it.

I'd driven by myself to Valley Forge for the class, an adventure in and of itself. I was ready for a shift, and I got one. While I was there,

I was also brave enough to look up a local Tae Kwon Do studio so I could get a workout in.

"Hi, my name is Laura, and I'm visiting from the D.C. area. I wondered if it would be okay to come take a class while I'm here this week?" I asked the young girl who answered the phone.

Even then, I didn't know if I'd have the guts to show up to a strange dojang, with strange people in a strange town I had never been to. I showed up and was welcomed. They practiced ITF (International Taekwondo Federation) forms! Amazing. It was a great class, and I had an amazing week. A week of healing.

And then I was diagnosed with a lipoma in my right upper arm. Lipoma means fatty lump of unknown origin. When it began growing in my arm, I first thought I was developing fantastic-looking triceps. Most people who saw it made a comment about it as well. In other words, it was that big.

I had the plastic surgeon at my dermatologist's office take a look at it after it started to get annoying and painful. It had been around for about a year already with the name "awesome triceps."

I really like my regular dermatologist. She was a she, and for me that worked better. She was kind and listened and did what she needed to do to deal with my needle phobia.

When you have skin like mine and a California-girl childhood in an age of Banana Boat deep tanning oil, you have a problem, and it's usually called basal cell carcinoma.

I had already had two Mohs procedures before I met this particular doctor and was tired of adding episodes to my already PTSD psyche.

Mohs procedures are done when you have a skin cancer that's specifically on your face. First, imagine a large needle in your face, then they cut out the offending tissue and go look at it right away under a microscope while you sit bleeding, with a huge bandage on your face, in the waiting room. They do this so that if they didn't get it all, you can go back into the procedure room and they'll cut more, rather than having to come back weeks later after a lab analyzes it, which is what they do for any other skin cancer that they remove at the dermatologist's office.

This new doctor was thorough, wanting to see me every six months, and when she found a spot to remove, I never felt the needles. Hallelujah!

When my triceps tumor got big, I had her look at it, and she recommended that I see the plastic surgeon on staff, telling me that the regular dermatologists didn't deal with stuff that big. So I reluctantly made what resulted in another "removal" appointment.

The plastic surgeon (male, strike one) explained, "I see these all the time. I'll numb up the arm and pop it out, fifteen minutes max."

I thought that sounded splendid and showed up for the procedure the following week.

A very kind friend of mine brought me to the visit. I hadn't wanted to bother my husband to take a day off of work with what I figured was going to be a half-hour procedure.

I was brought back to the procedure room, which I swear was no warmer than thirty-five degrees, with sweaty palms. My needle phobia was kicking in full force, even though I'd practiced breathing and relaxing in the waiting room.

Five long needles later (strike two), I did not feel the area around my lump. That was all the preparation I got. I was wide awake, fully conscious and aware of the scalpel that then dug through my upper arm.

It didn't hurt, but it was like my body reacted to the pain anyway. As he started to saw at the arm with his knife (really, I could see him sawing back and forth like when your steak knife is too dull), I began having a full visceral reaction: my body broke out in a sweat, I began to feel as if I would pass out (wouldn't that have been nice), and I got nauseous.

My legs then began to move like I was running. I told the nurse how I was feeling. "Hold still," she said.

And all of a sudden, "I can feel that!" I said, as loudly as I could muster to get their attention. I'm really not sure how many more times they stuck me with needles to continue numbing deeper into the tissue, three maybe.

Strike three. I was so done.

An hour and fifteen minutes later (so much for the quick fifteen I was promised), he sewed me up and shooed me out. I'm sure I had screwed up his whole schedule that day.

Miércoles! Why me?

The incision was about three inches long and healed up okay, but from the first week of recovery, I knew, I could *feel*, that he didn't get it all out. I pretended I didn't know.

The lump slowly began to grow back over the next several months. Shit, shit, shit. My arm started to hurt when I was treating patients, and I started to lean into my left arm during push-ups. Not good.

Deep breath. Here's the good stuff. I'm smiling now because I get to tell you the best healing story ever. For me anyway.

Dr. Mami Martin was recommended to me by a long-time client/friend who is many people's go-to person if they need a recommendation. My friend finds the best people. She won't settle for less, and she speaks up as needed.

"Okay, Cathy, I will call Dr. Martin," I promised.

I showed up at Dr. Martin's office both skeptical and hopeful. *Would someone be able to do this right,* I wondered.

She listened to my story, all of it, felt my lump, and then continued to explain everything. How the lump was rather big and should not have grown back in a year. How there can be pieces left behind from the first attempt that are causing that to happen. She explained she would never remove a lump that big without putting the person under general anesthesia first, and that way it would be quick and simple.

If she could make sure all the pieces were gone, I should have a very good result. I got up the nerve to tell my needle tale, but my eyes teared up. "My husband has the exact same problem," she said, putting my mind and heart at ease. She understood it. She was confident, she talked, she listened, we laughed a little, she educated me. And a small part of me healed that day. I scheduled the second procedure for three weeks later.

I had three weeks to think and maybe cancel. Maybe I could just live with it if it didn't get any bigger. Would the experience of the IV and general anesthesia just add to my surgery-related PTSD? *What if I died on the table?* Yeah, I thought that.

I didn't cancel. I began to wonder if this could be an opportunity for me to have a different sort of experience. An opportunity to heal. I wondered and imagined the best possible scenario. I got excited about it being done right.

One of my amazingly wonderful clients asked me if I was anxious about the upcoming procedure, and I ended up spilling my guts about being afraid of the IV needle, general anesthesia, and being sick afterward. This very smart client told me about things they can do these days to help with all of that and suggested I call the surgeon to talk to her about my worries.

Talk? To my surgeon? Like, call her on the phone and actually talk to her? Wow, can you do that? Oh my God!

So I called, and after three days of phone tag, she woke me up from a nap one afternoon. After complete and total anxiety-induced exhaustion, I'd passed out.

When I hung up the phone, I felt calm, not worried about the surgery but excited for it. Dr. Martin *listened* to my craziness and managed to not make me feel crazy. She joked with me on the phone. I bet you wish your surgeon could joke with you, too.

When I hung up the phone, I did not feel that normal pit-of-the-stomach worry or tight-and-anxious chest thing I was used to. I felt calm, grounded, and ready. I had a bit more healing that day, just from that conversation alone. I'd found a voice, and it was an effective one.

I continued to not worry the whole week leading up to surgery. I waited to feel the usual worry. It never came. I got in the car with my husband to drive to the hospital and even he asked me, "How are you doing?"

"Fine," I said. I meant it.

I ended up having some tears with the sweet Korean nurse that had to start my IV, but after letting her know how I was with needles, the tears dried up, and she was so fast I barely felt the needle.

Please, I beg all the blood drawers and IV starters of the world, go take lessons from my wonderful Korean nurse at Virginia Hospital Center.

The male anesthesiologist came in, and we talked. He also listened to my stories and was surprisingly interested in knowing about my experiences with feeling over-drugged and sick after general anesthesia. He even took the time to explain why that happens and why it wasn't going to happen that day.

He kept his promise. Not only did I not throw up when I woke, but I was hungry! Wow! Some kind woman brought me a whole extra bag of graham crackers and ginger ale when she saw me sucking out the crumbs from the graham cracker package.

The nurse who took care of me during wake-up time was funny, talking about her hair. She asked me how I was feeling and seemed to really care. "I'm a little dizzy," I told her.

A few minutes later, I let her know that the dizziness was gone. I sat there ready for the day to be done, hanging half out of my bed.

"Can I go home now?" I asked her.

"I was kind of hoping you would stick around," she joked, "It is nice to have an easy patient. Yes, let's get you your clothes and get you out of here."

That night, I took a pain pill, not because I had pain but because I wanted to be able to sleep. I never had pain. I went back to work four days after the procedure with no pain. I took my first Tae Kwon Do class six days after and had no pain.

My nurse client took a look at my arm that week, looked at me, and let me know that the kind of healing I had was out of the ordinary. Thanks, Dr. Martin. Thanks, Robin. Yay me!

Perfection of the Universe (I was conflicted the day I wrote this in my journal. I didn't know how to sort out my feelings about life after I had this particular conversation with a friend. I questioned many things, and I think that was good).

Journal entry May 22, 2011:

One of my good friends called me today to tell me that she does not believe in the perfection of the universe, that everything happens for a reason, that it is all meant to be. Specifically, she does not believe that being abused as a child was meant by God to be in her plan for a reason. How could it? How could a loving God put something as horrendous as that in our path? Another client of mine agrees, using 9/11 as an example: "How could 9/11 be anything but a random event? Meant to be? No, no, no, God did not just all of a sudden say, 'You, you, you, you, and you, done!'"

Hmm. I'm stuck on this one. I have always felt like life events happen before you, like someone laying the yellow brick road. Brick by brick, we eventually have a path before us. Sometimes the road splits and we have to make a decision to go this way or that, but sinking into the present moment, we can think back and say, "Wow, what would have happened had I gone left?" We can connect the bricks and feel they were put there for us.

I sat on the phone with my friend and couldn't think of how to respond. I believe in the perfection of the universe. That everything that comes our way is meant to be there. Meant to give us choices. That we can begin to see what is as just what is and leave out the judgements. No good or bad, right or wrong, just what is.

I like to help others believe it, too. How can I include those types of horrible things and not put an automatic judgement on them as bad? If everything is an opportunity for learning, for growth, or for healing, what would the opportunity in child abuse be? Some might say forgiveness. And 9/11? I'm not sure.

I thought about the fact that childhood abuse exists, later as an adult, only in our minds as a memory of past events. Healing most often happens when we become adults and can handle processing it. As adults, we're able to see the events of our past as our past, not current reality, and there could be opportunity for healing. What about the child who's being abused?

I cannot find the explanation there. In that moment, I can't see the perfection, learning, growth, or healing.

I believe we weren't meant to suffer. So what about when we do? To be alive means we'll get hurt, that we will fall. What counts is how fast we get up. Part of getting up fast is not identifying with what happened, not making it mean anything. Part of getting up fast is immediately letting go, not attaching.

Always present, always centered in the moment. If we are that, then we stay dynamic, spiritual beings without the baggage. Were we meant to suffer? Going back to the surfing metaphor, we won't always be riding on top, and that is okay because if we didn't crash, we wouldn't have the thrill of riding high on another wave.

My friend can't trust in the perfection of the universe because she was hurt so badly, and she has kept that hurt as part of who she is, stuck inside her mind and body, part of her identity. She can't center herself in the moment because if she does, then she has to feel her pain. It is unbearable.

When she moves through the wall of fire of her pain, only to reach the other side and realize that the wall was only a millimeter thick, she will see that she was meant to overcome, to survive, to live to tell the story, to heal. And that she isn't who she thought she was.

I think I still believe. What would our story be if it weren't true? Who would we be, and why would we be here? It is all meant to be. All the nastiness and evil. Otherwise, what would be the purpose? How would we truly know love and joy?

What matters is our reaction to the events of our lives. Our choices to go left or right on the path. What we do with what we have. What we make it mean. How we let it shape us. If we let it shape us. Our power and belief in our ability to shape our own world, despite the random things.

I think ultimately it's good to ask ourselves these big questions and compare our experiences and beliefs. In the grand scheme of things, this is all still a mystery. We really don't know what the right answer is, if there even is a right answer.

When we think we want to start teaching everyone what the right answer is, we ought to just close our mouths. Sometimes in my life, things feel like they are meant to be there, like fate.

Sometimes the events seem random.

I wonder what life would have been like if I had made a certain choice and ponder the possible outcomes. When I was twenty something, I was engaged to be married. The week we received the custom-printed wedding invitations in the mail, I caught him in bed with another woman.

I wonder what would have happened if I'd never caught him and we had gone through with the wedding. I shudder thinking about it. I marvel at what the actual events were and what they led to. For now, it's okay to not know all the answers. I have to be okay not knowing the answers and enjoying the mystery and the journey.

Think about the healing moments of your own life now. What's left to master?

In the next chapter, you'll read the story about earning a black belt, and how that was only the beginning.

What kind of healing has transformed your life? Is there anything left to work on?

Use these pages to record your thoughts about the questions at the beginning and end of this chapter...

Black Belt

*What is **your** black belt? And how are you going for it?*
This year, I wrote a book. I learned how to canter on a horse (and not fall off). I wrote and submitted two articles to a magazine and sent my book idea to a publisher. I created a new vision for my business. I took a marketing course. I tried, again, to learn how to reconcile my bank statements. Ugh.

I practiced being in the moment and feeling the anxiety. I read books about marketing, which would not be my first choice. I figured out how to be with my husband and talk to him without hiding or fighting. Hint: that was big for me.

I planned a big vacation to celebrate my dad's seventieth birthday. I am realizing that the end of my story is just the beginning. My black belt vision, as it manifests, just leaves possibility for more to come.

I watch my life unfold in front of me, and I'm wrapped up in it, aware of the details and paying attention to my vision. I can practice this every morning when my eyes open, beginning by being grateful, and all it takes is a shift in thinking.

A discipline of positive attitude and action helps me lean into the direction I want to go. Sometimes I get caught up in thoughts like, "I'm getting old," "Life is going too fast," "I don't have enough time to do all the things I want to do," or "Why didn't I start this sooner."

It's easy to do that to yourself. Really easy to let those kind of thoughts take over, get you down, and send all your positive, creative energy flow screeching to a halt. It takes some determination to make sure that doesn't happen. I have to choose the other path in each of my moments. And keep practicing.

Master Holloway announced the date of the black belt test during class on October 8. A date that marks the end of many years of practice, but the beginning of another chapter. Maybe even another book.

Journal entry October 9, 2011

Halfway through class, as we finished a kicking drill, Master Holloway casually said, "December 17th." We all looked up at him in that moment not totally sure what he was talking about. *One through seventeen? Is that what he said?*

I thought this as I looked side to side to see if my classmates knew what was going on.

"Black belt test December 17th," he repeated. I'm not totally sure what I felt in that moment. I had been waiting for that announcement for ten months. Six years and ten months, actually. I felt two things at once: caught by surprise and "it's about time" relieved.

I took a breath as he just as casually went on to the next drill. It feels like I have been waiting forever to hear those words. Now I fight some anxiety with it. I don't really want to be anxious for the next three months, so I begin to remind myself of how far I have come and my practice of staying present. It will serve me well in the next seventy days, the next 1,680 hours of my life where I will have a choice to practice disciplining my mind.

About a week after this announcement, Master Holloway called Jonathan and I over after class and let us know that there would be an extra test for the red belt kids and that to be eligible for the black belt test on December 17th, Jonathan would have to pass this pretest.

The pretest started at 2:00 p.m. on October 22nd, the afternoon of Danielle's birthday party. This would be the first ever test that I would not be able to fully attend. Imagine my brain being full of crazy thoughts at this point.

I drove Jonathan to the test and was able to watch about an hour-and-a-half of the four-and-a-half-hour test. His dad met us there and stayed for the rest so I could go home and start the festivities with my daughter. I hated leaving. I hated not being there. Every ounce of me wanted to see his sparring and his board breaking and anything else he did.

I texted his dad about twenty times in those couple hours. "How is he?" "Did he spar yet?" "Did he finish sparring?" "How did he do?" "Is he going to try three boards?" "WHAT HAPPENED?"

Oh my poor husband.

It turned out great. Jonathan fought hard, never gave up, and broke two boards with a back kick on his first try. I survived not being there for every single moment.

The girls at the party surprised him with a loud "Congratulations!" when he came in the door that night, and they had pizza and cake together. He was a rock star. Though he has been a rock star since he was born in *my* book.

This year has been a black belt kind of year. I have made some changes, I have used my voice, I've taken action, I've learned new things, and I've taught what I know.

I've cleared out and made space for something new and truer. I've peeled off the layers. It's about time.

What took me so long? What takes people a lifetime to figure things out? Why does it feel so important, this thing we have about making ourselves bigger?

Reaching out, feeling connected, being able to help, and changing things. Aren't we perfect just the way we are stuck?

That question makes me laugh. If I'm not aware that I'm feeling stuck, then life is perfect stuck. If I notice, then it matters. If I believe I have a choice to make it different, then it matters. If I have a vision of something better, then it matters.

So how did it come to matter for me?

Well, that's the story you have just read. I'm glad for it, for the adventure of it all, for the awareness. I believe ignorance is hell.

I felt at first that telling my story was my ego talking, even with the burning feeling of purpose behind it. A good friend of mine keeps telling me that ego is okay (necessary, even), that we don't survive without it. That it gets an undeserving bad rap.

My thought is that telling my story ultimately makes tiny shifts in the people reading the story, only in that they might think about something slightly differently than before. Or maybe it makes big shifts and that same person takes an action they wouldn't have otherwise risked. A movement through fear.

If ego wants me to tell my story and in doing so it helps someone, then I will be grateful for it instead of rejecting it. I can live with it, in awareness, and allow its lessons to make me into a bigger circle.

Another good friend says, "And maybe none of this matters." My Landmark Forum class taught us that "life is empty and meaningless, and the fact that it's empty and meaningless is empty and meaningless."

Chew on that for a moment, and feel the space you just made for *anything* you want in your life.

So we can tell our stories, or not. We can be big or small. We can take a risk or keep ourselves quietly in our comfort zone. We can speak or be silenced. We can try something new or just dream of doing it. We can teach what we know, or we can keep it to ourselves for fear of someone stealing it. We can do whatever we want to do. It really is about making our own choices. And it is all good. Really.

Black Belt Essay December 17, 2011:

Thank you, Master Holloway...
I'm strong enough to start a leaf blower, lawn mower, and just about any other power tool.

I know how to block a kick, and more importantly, I know how to take a kick and survive.
I'm fast enough to get out of the way of a kick, a moving car, and a 1,000-pound horse.

I know it's okay to be afraid as long as I do something about it.
I know that if I can stay relaxed, I will be better.

I will be better for the mistakes I make.
Just because I can't do something doesn't mean I won't be able
to if I try and practice.

I know that teaching someone to do something makes you learn it
better.
I know that how you act counts; you never know who is looking up
to you.

I'm tall enough at 5'3" to score at the head of almost anyone.
I know that getting hurt doesn't mean you quit.
I learned that just being with someone is enough; you don't
always have to say anything.

I learned that allowing someone to figure something out, rather
than always giving them the answer, helps them learn.
I figured out that slowing down gives you time for the answers to
come by themselves.

I'm brave enough to do most anything.

I'm smart enough to do what I want to do, and not what everyone
else wants me to do.

I'm lucky to have had great teachers in my life.
I can break a lot of wood with my foot!
I know that Tae Kwon Do is in everything I do; it is a way of being.
I know that I want to teach this to whoever wants to learn it, for as
long as there are people to teach.
I have a voice, and it is okay to use it.
I have something to give.
My life is a gift, and its purpose is to share it.

This year has been one of tremendous growth for me. Convinced I have been going through what everyone calls a midlife crisis. Questioning everything about my marriage, family, purpose in life...like being in the middle of an earthquake (which I have actually been in the middle of before), the shit is falling off the walls and ceiling all around you, and you have to keep getting out of the way so you don't get beamed—or worse. Then everything is calm and quiet, and you are sitting in the middle of all the shit, paralyzed, until you decide that you have been sitting there long enough and that you had better get your ass up and start cleaning because there are things to be done. Okay, done with the swear words.

Life is like an earthquake, or maybe more like a roller coaster, and I'm convinced now that part of the secret to life is being the one who can raise her hands in the air and scream bloody murder until you are laughing so hard you pee your pants.

Why go on the ride otherwise? Why go on it if you are going to close your eyes, grip the bar so tight that you can't feel your hands after a minute, clench every part of your body up every time the car moves you up or down, and then vow to never ride again?

The problem in life is you have to ride. You have no real choice. It's how you ride that counts. The ups are full of excitement and anticipation. The downs leave your stomach emptied and wondering "what the hell?" You can think you know what the ups and downs are going to be like, what to do to prepare for them, how many ups there will be, and if you deserve more of them or not. You can think about and judge the ups and downs all you want. Fact is the ride will go on, and it is fairly short. Riding in fear just sucks. Riding silent sucks. Riding with a death grip sucks. Never knowing just how loud you can scream? What a shame.

A very good friend of mine swallowed a bottle of pills this year. Caused an earthquake in her life and in all those who love her. She was riding the roller coaster in her silent death grip for a really long time. This friend, a sane, responsible, professional, giving friend. She gave and gave and gave to everyone else but herself. Then she got so angry, she cracked. What a mess. She is now, having survived, figuring out what to do with all the shit around her. What the hell?

I examined my life since then, all the ups and downs, and had a profound sense of gratitude. How am I so lucky? It made all the things I'd been complaining about seem stupid. STUPID.

My heart opened up a little, and I felt softer. I'd been riding with my hands up for sure, but just a little clenched, not screaming loud enough. We can't be afraid to scream, loud enough for someone to hear it and respond to it. Directly enough so others know what you are screaming about.

Why are we afraid to let go like that? My midlife crisis suddenly was put into perspective, and something shifted in me. The ride took a hard turn. Life is short. We all have to take the ride. Making a choice to end the ride yourself; I don't think it's that simple. Better to choose how you take the ride to begin with.

I'll never forget the year we took the kids to Hershey Park (an actual roller coaster story). Danielle was trying to get her nerve up to ride one of the roller coasters with Jonathan and me. She said yes, and off we went.

I watched her beside me, the look on her face when after the long ascent, the car let go and our stomachs dropped out. The look was terror, almost at tears. Then up we went again, and she looked at me with those watery eyes.

I shouted at her over the sound of the clicks of the track as we went up the second time, "Scream as loud as you can!"

"What?" she said.

"SCREAM AS LOUD AS YOU CAN!" I screamed.

The car dropped out from under us. We screamed and screamed all the way down. When I was able to turn and look at her, all I saw was a smile.

"Can we do that again?" she asked.

What we do with fear can make the difference in our lives. The difference between truly living and living in a silent death grip. We're afraid of hurting people, of what they will say, of what they will do; we are afraid of looking bad or sounding stupid; we're afraid of failure, of losing, of being rejected. We're afraid of change, and of staying the same, of getting sick, of dying, of living.

We are all afraid.

In my crisis this year, I questioned my identity, my sexuality, my purpose, my worth. I could create joy and passion in all the areas of my life, except my primary relationship. Failure. Fear crept in.

What am I doing here? What the hell? Is this a test? Am I supposed to take care of everyone else first? Me first? My friend chose a bottle of pills. Does it all have to be so serious? When can we have a little fun?

One big difference in my life is that my roller coaster ride had a Tae Kwon Do loop. I'm so lucky I got to punch and kick and yell for the last six years, thank God. Not only that, but I got to punch and kick actual people, legally, and nobody reprimanded me for yelling; in fact, the louder, the better.

Really, where else can you kick people and scream and not get sent to the principal's office or put in jail?

I'm so very grateful that the day my six-year-old son said about Tae Kwon Do, "Mom, I will go if you do too," I replied, "Okay!"

Here we are these years later, with our black belts, and really so much more than that...so much more.

This ride has been awesome, and now I look forward to giving back, teaching, learning more, and continuing the journey. If something as great as this could appear in my life when it did (at age 38), then who knows what other cool things are in store.

I keep riding, with my hands up, and wait for what's next. Hands up and screaming all the way, that's a choice I'll have to remake every day, because the fear creeps in sometimes. The difference since Tae Kwon Do is that I'm starting to learn what to do when I feel it.

Before, it only felt like a wall that stopped me. Now I know I can use it and do something with it to make it work for me. Being less attached to the outcome of what I do, I can feel fear but act anyway, just to see what happens. This might be the difference between going through the motions of life and really living out loud in joy and passion. That's a gift better than any I've ever received.

Many thanks and love to you, Master Holloway, for being the one who keeps giving this gift to me. These words will never truly express my gratitude to you and Master M for always asking us to be our best and to move through the fear to reach our goals, and for riding this ride with us.

At this point, I've visualized myself as a black belt, behaved like a black belt, and written my black belt essay. The only thing left was to finally earn that belt.

How are you taking action toward your vision? What small thing can you do today to lean toward your dreams?

Use these pages to record your thoughts about the questions at the beginning and end of this chapter...

Chapter One

*W*hat if you considered every day a new beginning? How would you start your journey?

The chapters of Living, Healing and Tae Kwon Do that you've just read were written before the black belt test on December 17, 2011, except for the first journal entry written that very morning. This last chapter, that I'm calling "Chapter One," is my best tale of the black belt test.

I've been waiting excitedly to write this chapter, to finish this book with a story of triumph and a result that comes from healing, dedication, love, and passion. This's a chapter that's a beginning, not an end.

Saturday, December 17, 2011, 7:10 a.m.:

I've been thinking I should feel different, be different after this test somehow. I know better. What I do or achieve is not who I am. So I'm stuck with a feeling of, why does this matter? Not does it matter, but why, because it matters!

Because even though the things we do and achieve and the roles we play are not who we are, we serve our highest purpose through them. So that is why. I found something that by expressing myself through it has allowed me to live in passion, which is the best expression of myself I can give to the world. I love this stuff, and it matters to me, which means it benefits others. That might be the only reason we ever need.

Today's going to be a great day. I love you, Jonathan, and am proud beyond words to be by your side today.

Six-and-a-half hours of magnificently intense, excruciating, fantastic, fighting, love, determination, and family. These are some mediocre words to start you off with to describe the amazing experience I had that day. It was everything I'd hoped for, with a couple extra surprises.

I can't stop thinking about it. Images and sounds of the day keep running through my brain, playing themselves over and over, and I don't get tired of it.

Today, I'm re-feeling every hug I got yesterday. I've smiled ten times over when I relive the cheer that went up in that room when Master Holloway announced that Jonathan and I were now first-degree black belts. My eyes tear up every time I think about the moment my son, in pure let-down happiness, buried his head in my arm for a hug and burst into tears. Yeah, buddy, I know; I feel the same way.

I want to tell you everything about that day.

Our friend from class, Peter, picked Jonathan and I up at the house so we could all ride together to the test. Thank you, Peter, because I'm now not sure if my legs would have been able to gas and brake for the drive home.

It was marvelous to have the company on the drive, as that period of time in past tests always seems to be the absolute worst for me, as far as pretest anxiety goes. So we drove and talked, and I was nicely distracted from the way my stomach felt. And speaking of my stomach? Not good. Had to force breakfast down and could only eat half of my planned, super-powered lunch.

Peter, having earlier admitted to me that he was equally paranoid about being to the dojang on time, got us there perfectly early. Thank you again, Peter. Big sigh of relief.

I'd brought my iPod so I could listen to my Tae Kwon Do mix for some pumping-up action. I normally do this in my car on the way to a test so nobody has to listen to me sing Van Halen at the top of my lungs.

Since I had a ride this time, that wasn't going to work, so I listened to *Jump* and *Dynamite* and a few other good songs while Jonathan and I sat and stretched and warmed ourselves up. It was good.

More people started arriving (after the anally early people came the normal, on-time people), and I put Van Halen away so I could join the rest of my friends for some nervous warm-up chatter.

I watched as all of our friends came in to join us, feeling happy as I saw each familiar face and smile, the comrades who would do this thing with us today.

"Line up!" we finally heard, and formed rows of four across the room. I think there were nineteen of us total and later found out that two of them would not be staying to complete the test, so in the end there were seventeen.

"Class! Cha Rutt! Kyung Yet!" Master Lee did a fantastic "Cha Rutt, Kyung Yet," the loudest I have ever heard.

I had a quick goosebumps reaction in that moment. Loved it. We warmed up with kicks and then got down to business. Nerves had diminished 90 percent at this point. Getting physical always helps.

Basic kicks had to be in time with the group. We didn't do a good enough job the first go-around, so he split us into two groups and did it again. Most of us were in a full sweat at this point.

Forms started with Jonathan, who was called out by himself. In random order (which is harder), he was asked to perform each one. If he faltered or messed up, he repeated it.

This might have been the first mom reaction I felt inside of me, just wanting him to feel good about what he was doing. I mentally followed each move of his forms and knew when he was off but watched proudly as he picked up where he needed to and kept going.

I could hear two others behind me as we all whispered "that's it" when he would get himself back on track.

I realized then that I wasn't the only mom in the room, and in that moment, I felt the family that stood around me, that was there for me and my son. What a fantastic, indescribable feeling. I couldn't help being a mom, but I had incredible back-up that night.

Then it was my turn to do the same. I had to get my side kicks to stick. Eventually, most of them did. Then forms as a group. The black belts were called to the side to watch the rest of us perform each form as a group. They each had one of us red belts to watch and give feedback to, and then we repeated the form to see if we could fix what we were told needed fixing.

Thank you, Master Lee, for all the tips. Then each of the red belts had to perform their highest form, Choong-Moo, solo. The black belt group then did all of their forms as a group. We did a lot of forms.

One of my favorite parts of a test is watching the black belt group as they complete at least nine more forms past the nine that the red belts know, and do it in sync for the most part. It's beautiful to watch, like a dance. It's hard to believe that a person can remember that many forms, one after the other, without missing a beat, but this group does just that. Love it!

Not sure if I remember the order of events perfectly at this point, but I think one-steps were next. There are ten one-step maneuvers that we (at least some of us) have memorized. Those who haven't memorized the moves are led by those of us who have, which is a good way to teach them.

I'd worked on these and had them all down. That was not the case on the last test. Brett grabbed me as his partner, which was great because we had practiced together in class the same week, and off we went through each ten.

"Get your pads on," is what we heard next. Sparring might be the hardest part of the test. I take that back; for sure it is, because by this time we are getting a little tired, and sparring takes a mind-body effort. It takes all you have left. And you have to find something left, because about halfway through sparring, you could swear there is nothing left to give. Not one more kick. I wondered at one point if my foot was going to lift off the ground one more time, never mind actually kick above the knee.

We sparred in pairs as a group, rotating through, for a long time. I think those are two-minute rounds. We line up in two rows facing each other. We take up the entire length of the room at this point and have to deal with sparring our partner and staying out of the way of our neighbors' kicks too.

I'm pretty sure I stepped on and/or kicked someone who was not my partner at least three times. Then Master Lee called out a few pairs at a time, maybe three pairs, and that group went. Jonathan did this for a while. And this's when the mom in me had a hard time. I knew that this part of the test would be difficult, for him, for me, for all of us. And it was fine.

He fought his little heart out, sometimes through tears, at one point through sobs, and then rallied and fought pretty frickin' hard in the end, with some nice kihaps.

The entire room cheered him on. The entire room, folks! Family.

Thank you, guys and gals, for cheering on my son like he was yours. You are all first class in my book. Thank you to those who gave me a look of recognition during those moments, too. A look that said, "I know how you are feeling, and it will be okay."

As we went through the rotation of sparring, Jonathan and I were not allowed to be out of the line-up. So, no breaks. That was tough. I felt sick and was hurting in several places that I can't remember enough to list right now. And I kept going, finding the something left.

Even though you are feeling the pure physical exhaustion at this point, you realize a lot of it is in your mind. You have to stop thinking "tired" and figure out some other thing to tell yourself.

"This will be over soon," "Only two minutes left," "This is all in my head," "This is your time to shine," "Find what you have left," are all encouragements I used.

It mostly worked. The support from my friends helped tremendously. Thank you, Diego, for the "pace yourself" speech. I knew that but wasn't doing it. To all of you who encouraged me with your words, thank you very much.

Sparring continued with first Jonathan and then me having to take on the entire group of black belts, one by one, for one-minute rounds, no stopping. This is when you really think, *I got nothing left,* but have to find some anyway.

There are really very few appropriately descriptive words for how proud I felt about my son during this time. I'm going to repeat myself now: this is hard. It is also what makes you be able to stand up at the head of the room at the end and know you just earned that beautiful black belt you are sporting.

If you had doubts about whether or not you earned it before, you do not have any doubts left after this round of sparring. You just don't. It's magnificent. And you're sparring among the cheers, encouragement, and suggestions of your friends, who have been there. You know they know how you feel. You know they want you to succeed. You know they need you to succeed, that your success is theirs.

Then it's over.

And then you have to break a f@#$%ng board. Or six, in my case. Because that's what my little brain came up with the week before the test. It was actually supposed to be seven (ending with a hammer fist technique that I'd never had the nerve to try before), but I took the seventh board out of the routine at the last minute, out of sheer, oh-my-God-what-have-I-done panic.

I was so sick to my stomach at this point that for a moment I had a thought that I might have to lie down. I rallied, ate a GU gummy chew or two, and experienced a slight increase in blood sugar that might have helped. The sickness passed. Thank you, God.

(I'm fairly sure a few people talked to me during this waiting period, and I just want to say to them now that I apologize if I said something totally spacey or if I didn't answer you at all!)

Nerves aside, breaking is my other favorite part of Tae Kwon Do. There's something so totally cool about being able to do this. Being able to break (six different boards) at the end of a black belt test is beyond totally cool. It's ridiculous. Fantastically ridiculous that we can make ourselves find the power, accuracy, and speed it takes to break those boards, especially at the very end of a test when we are completely spent.

Jonathan went before me, with a back kick to three boards, a first attempt for him. He got it on the third try. My routine included a reverse turning kick to one board, a step side kick to two boards and a jump side to three boards. The first two were a breeze.

I couldn't break the three boards with my jump side, so I changed my mind and switched to a jump back kick and broke them on the second try! There is just nothing like this. You really ought to try it some time.

We watched each of our colleagues finish their awesome breaking routines and cheered after each one. Their success was mine. Somehow, the energy is connected in that room. Everyone is quiet in anticipation of a break, feeling the focus of the student, feeling it in themselves, and feeling the triumph when they succeed. You get to feel your own victory, and then you get to feel it sixteen more times. Love it!

Then it was time to clean up the floor, clear the boards, sweep up the tiny wood shards, and line up. "Sit down," we heard Master Holloway say.

A collective moan was shared as we all managed to get our cramped-up, bruised bodies down to the floor. It was surmised that the average age in that room, if you took out Jonathan at eleven and Maggie at seventeen, was probably forty-five years. The moaning was a giveaway. I will tell you that this is an especially fit group of forty- to sixty-year-olds who will be forever young by continuing this sport.

As Master Holloway called their names, the red belts each moved to the front of the room and received their stripes. The black belt degree promotions were next.

Three of my friends from the YMCA received their second-degree promotion. There was a fourth-degree promotion, two fourth-degree, third-class promotions, and then a pause.

Jonathan, me, and Lois were left.

"Jonathan!" The vibration of Master Holloway's voice moved my heart.

Master Holloway called Jonathan up to the front and shook his hand while he talked to him about this day being a beginning of the next phase for him.

Then I was called up to stand next to my son. A moment I'd dreamt about. It felt like I thought it would, like one of the most incredible moments of my life.

Master Holloway announced our promotion to first-degree black belt, and the room erupted in cheers! Wow! I had goose-bumps again. Master Holloway stepped away for a moment at that point to retrieve our new black belt uniforms. I turned to Jonathan, leaned down, and asked him if I could give him a hug now (he wouldn't let me earlier).

As he nodded without speaking, his face began to scrunch up into a cry, and he buried his head into my arm for a hug as the tears fell. I heard someone behind us say, "Those are happy tears!" I knew it too. He came up for a breath and then came back in for a second hug. Ah. I was a mom—a black belt mom—hugging her eleven-year-old black belt son, and I honestly can't describe the feeling. Overwhelming.

Jonathan and I were handed our new uniforms and asked to go change as the rest of the group waited. We came out onto the floor decked out in our crispy new white-and-black uniforms and marvelously new black belts to the whistles and smiles of our friends. It's really hard not to have a crazy big smile on your face at that point.

Lois was the last to be promoted, to fifth-degree black belt. An incredible end to our day. In the company of wisdom, experience, and love. Jonathan and I ran through the gauntlet of our peers for high fives and then faced the group for a final "Cha Rutt! Kyung Yet!" Each of the new degreed black belts did the same.

Tradition. Respect. We took many pictures afterward. Great pictures, lots of smiles and hugs all around. I can still feel each of those hugs today, my friends. Thank you.

Journal entry December 20, 2011, 7:30 p.m.

From Black to White. I knew part of the black belt test was to teach the next class I showed up at. I was so exhausted last night that I hoped Jonathan wouldn't want to go, a feeling I have never had before. No such luck.

A chance to show off those beautiful new uniforms and belts was just too good to pass up. When David started the class, I thought I was off the hook. Master Holloway came into class about twenty minutes into it, stopped everything, and had me take over. Ugh.

I took over, no problems, no issues, but felt like a total idiot. I felt small. I felt like a white belt again, only this time I was being tested.

I love teaching, but I hated it last night. I'm a pretty good teacher, but last night you could have said I was the best teacher ever and I wouldn't have believed you.

What was that horrible feeling I felt last night? Where did that come from? Could anyone else tell? I even asked the kids in the car out of sheer desperation if they thought I did okay. "You did fine," they said.

I believed them but felt the awful feelings anyway. I was shoved off of cloud nine face-first and left to survive alone with my feelings. I had some perspective given to me the next day, as I realized that nobody died. I'm not totally sure perspective matters too much when you are in the middle of your own chaos, but I think it helped slightly.

Today, I continue to feel the effects of the test: total exhaustion. Still sleepy and unable to catch up. Really sad and grumpy, kind of PMS-like. Still a little "sick." Weird feeling. Like, burnt. I can feel my body and my mind still trying to recover.

After the holiday break, the kids and I returned to class all together for the first time. It was spectacular to arrive and hear "Congratulations!" from our classmates. We went through the usual warm-up and kicks, and then it was time to practice our forms.

Master Holloway came over to Jonathan and me, and we began learning Kwang-Gae, our first black belt form. I smiled, with

Jonathan beside me, as I felt a surge of the same amazing feelings I had had six years prior when we had our very first Tae Kwon Do class. I loved this stuff!

We practiced the new moves of Kwang-Gae over and over without tiring, excited to be learning a new form after two years of Choong-Moo, our red belt form. I felt like a beginner again and loved every second of it. So much behind us, and a whole new world ahead.

That is my Tae Kwon Do!

It feels right and hard to start all over again. With the basics behind me, I feel excited to teach. With so much ahead of me, I'm eager to move faster. I'm honored to have the mentors around me who've been there, people who care about this just as much as I do and understand my crazy passion.

I yearn to be that mentor for someone else. I have come so far, learned and accomplished so much. I have felt healing and transformation. There is so much still to discover.

The vulnerability I felt when my kids were born has changed. I can tolerate the feelings of it without being hopeless and fearful. Instead, I am empowered and can speak up and act in the face of that fear. I feel inspired to continue to speak and act for my children, and for myself, because I am now aware of the cost of being silent.

Being aware and having a choice makes the difference. Dreams have manifested before my eyes. I would like to teach others what I know!

What now? How do I best serve? When do I start? What do I do? How do I continue to make my work my play and live in my passions? Can I inspire others to do the same?

Right now, I take a deep breath, remember where I'm sitting, listen to the sounds of my home and my family around me and type this last sentence being okay with not knowing what is next.

How will you make sure to enjoy the journey?

Use these pages to record your thoughts about the questions at the beginning and end of this chapter, and enjoy your journey!

Resources

Websites
Brave Healer Productions: www.BraveHealer.com
Gentle East Taekwondo: www.GentleEast.com
International Taekwondo Federation: https://www.taekwondoitf.org/
John F. Barnes Myofascial Release: www.MyofascialRelease.com
CranioSacral Therapy: www.Upledger.com

Books
Adyashanti. *True Meditation.* Boulder, CO: Sounds True, Inc., 2006.
Bacci, Ingrid. *The Art of Effortless Living.* New York: The Berkley Publishing Group, 2000.
Barnes, John F. *Healing Ancient Wounds.* Paoli, PA: Rehabilitation Services, Inc., 2000.
Beckwith, Michael Bernard. *Spiritual Liberation.* New York: Atria Books,, 2008.
Byrne, Rhonda. *The Secret.* New York: Atria Books, 2006.
Byrne, Rhonda. *The Power.* New York: Atria Books, 2010.
Dooley, Mike. *Manifesting Change.* New York: Atria Paperback, 2011.
Duerk, Judith. *Circle of Stones.* Philadelphia: Innisfree Press, Inc., 1989.
Dyer, Dr. Wayne W. *Excuses Begone!.* Carlsbad, CA: Hay House, Inc., 2009.
Oriah. *The Invitation.* New York: HarperCollins Publishers, 1999.

Scurlock-Durana, Suzanne. *Full Body Presence*. Novato, CA: Nataraj Publishing, 2010.

Tolle, Eckhart. *A New Earth*. New York: Penguin Books, 2006.

About the Author

Laura Di Franco, MPT, is the owner of Brave Healer Productions and a powerhouse who writes to Feng Shui her soul. She's a six-time published poet and author, inspirational speaker, holistic physical therapist, and third-degree black belt in Tae Kwon Do with almost three decades of experience in healing. She was born to build a revolution of brave healers who are getting their badass, authentic voices published in order to heal the world with their words. She and her son earned their black belts on December 17, 2011. Laura still lives in Maryland and practices Tae Kwon Do at Gentle East Taekwondo with Master Holloway. You can find her online at www.BraveHealer.com.

You'll find all Laura's books on Amazon:
Brave Healing: A Guide for Your Journey (Burke, VA: Possibilities Publishing Company, 2018)
Warrior Love: A Journal to Inspire Your Fiercely Alive Whole Self
Warrior Joy: A Journal to Inspire Your Fiercely Alive Whole Self
Warrior Soul: a Journal to Inspire Your Fiercely Alive Whole Self
Warrior Dreams: A Journal to Inspire Your Fiercely Alive Whole Self

You'll find Laura at www.BraveHealer.com;
On Facebook @kickasswarriorgoddess;
On Instagram @BraveHealerbyLaura;
On Twitter @LiveHealTKD;
And in her free Facebook group: The Brave Healers Mastermind and Refuge.

Thank you so much for reading this book. I hope I've inspired your inner warrior! I'd be incredibly grateful if you'd take just a few minutes and leave a review of the book on Amazon, which will help others looking for books that inspire! And don't hesitate to head over to BraveHealer.com and fill out that contact form, drop me a line and tell me how you liked the book!

Made in the USA
Middletown, DE
14 July 2019